LAPSTRAKE CANOES

Everything You Need to Know to Build a Light, Strong, Beautiful Boat

David L. Nichols

BREAKAWAY BOOKS
HALCOTTSVILLE, NEW YORK
2007

Lapstrake Canoes:
Everything You Need to Know to Build a Light, Strong, Beautiful Boat

Text, photos, and illustrations copyright © 2007 by David L. Nichols

First page photo credits:
Top two photos: © 2007 by G. Bair Carlson-Duchman
Canoe sailing: © 2007 by Linda O'Krent

ISBN: 978-1-891369-72-8
Library of Congress Control Number: 2007925652

Published by Breakaway Books
P.O. Box 24
Halcottsville, NY 12438
www.breakawaybooks.com
Printed in China

FIRST EDITION

ACKNOWLEDGEMENTS

I would like to thank my son, Harlan Nichols, for his tireless help with this book, and my daughter, Simone Nichols, for her excellent editorial advice. They make their father proud.

Contents

For my wife, Candy—without her unending support and encouragement this book wouldn't be.

Introduction

My main influence when I designed the boats in this book was the decked double-paddle canoes from the late 1880s and early 1900s. Many of those canoes, like John MacGregor's Rob Roy, made very impressive voyages, and it was the books written about his voyages that helped popularize this type of canoe in Europe and this country. American canoe builders like J. Henry Rushton, R. J. Douglas, and others built a variety of lovely cedar-planked as well as lapstrake designs, and those designs carried American canoeists on adventures large and small.

The canoes in this book are also lapstrake, but there is a difference: My designs use glued lapstrake construction rather than traditional lapstrake construction. Glued lapstrake construction is far less labor intensive and is a more forgiving method. This means your boat will be on the water faster and doesn't require the high skill level of the traditional lapstrake boats, but you still get that traditional look.

Also, I designed all three of these canoes to be extremely user friendly and stable—stable enough to stand in. That means getting in and out of these canoes is an easy matter and doesn't require the agility of an acrobat. This is an important consideration because the boat you choose to build should be a pleasure to use as well as simple to construct.

In addition, you'll find that this book is written for someone who has little or no knowledge of boatbuilding. It will take you through each step of the building process in great detail. You'll find instructions for making a downwind sail and a fine double paddle as well. So, if you have a desire to build a boat and you have this book, then you have all you need to build three beautiful, sea-kindly canoes.

If you have built boats before and have a good knowledge base, then feel free to skip to the back; there you'll find the tables of offsets and station spacing for all three boats. And that, of course, is all you need.

Whatever your experience level, the designs in this book are well tested and will serve you well for years to come. Enjoy!

1

Getting Started

Boats, particularly small boats, are like magic carpets. They can carry you on adventures large and small. And like the magic carpet you roll up and store until the next adventure, the small boat can be stored in an out-of-the-way place until that time when you are ready to, like Huck Finn, strike out for "the territory ahead."

The three boats in this book are made for the Territory Ahead, whether it's a close-by pond or a vast wilderness like the Boundary Waters Canoe Area. But unlike the impossible-to-own magic carpet, these boats are easy to build and therefore easy to own.

There is nothing magical or difficult about building a boat. It's just one step after another until you are ready to launch your boat . . . your magic carpet.

Probably the two biggest problems facing the first-time builder—or any builder for that matter—are finding the space and finding the time. So the good news is, any of the boats in this book can be built on one side of a double-car garage and in less time than you might think.

The other nice thing about small boats, and these in particular, is that they can be built with simple hand tools. It's not necessary to own a complete woodworking shop; the tools listed here will do the job very well. If you don't own them all, and can't buy them all, think of friends, neighbors, and relatives who might loan some out for a good cause.

Saber saw with fine-tooth blades
Block plane
Drill and bits (cordless drill best)
¾-inch chisel
Screwdrivers
Hand saw (Japanese saw best)
Clamps (10 minimum)
Hammer (small will be best)
Electric sander (5-inch random orbital sander)
Tape measure at least 16 feet long
36- to 48-inch rule with straight edge
Level
Square
Dust mask and safety glasses
Mat knife or razor blades
Coarse wood rasp

Helpful additional tools:

Table saw
8-inch jack plane
Belt sander and frame (for scarfing and finishing small parts)
Circular saw (for scarfing alternative)
Router (for scarfing alternative and trim jobs)
Power plane (for scarfing alternative)
Tapered drill bits and countersinks
Rabbet plane
Japanese keyhole saw
Japanese flush-cut trim saw
Crank-leg chisel

Figure 1-1

The first major step in the process will be to build a strongback and set up the station molds. **Figure 1-1** shows the strongback (this is the foundation for your boat) with the station molds and bulkheads (this is the framework or the skeleton for your boat) set up at the appropriate places.

Figure 1-2

The next major step is to plank your boat. In **Figure 1-2** Little Princess, the 12-foot-long solo canoe, has her bottom, garboard, and sheer plank in place and is ready to turn over.

Figure 1-3

Figure 1-3 shows Little Princess turned over with her deck in place and trimmed. At this stage she's ready for the outwales, inwales, and the rest of her interior.

It took about 80 hours to get her to this point, although some builders will take longer. But about half of that work can be done before you ever set up the strongback and station molds. This means that if demands for the building space require it, the boat can be assembled and pulled off the strongback in a couple of long three-day weekends. Then with space cleaned up and Little Princess stored out of the way, the car can be moved back into the garage.

This assumes, of course, that you're working efficiently and without mistakes. However, it might be best if first-time builders didn't set unrealistic timetables for finishing the boat. The building process should be enjoyed—not viewed as a chore that must be slogged though as quickly as possible. Even for the builder who wishes to build at a leisurely pace, doing much of the work in advance will make the process smoother and launch day arrive sooner.

The builders who rush through to launch will miss many of the pleasures that make boatbuilding a joy. They will never allow themselves to experience the feel of a finely tuned plane as it shaves a paper-thin curl of wood; even gnarly old boatbuilders smile slightly when they describe that feeling. They will miss the meditative calm that comes from sitting quietly at the end of a work session and admiring the lines of their boat.

Each boat has a sweet spot, a place where all the lines seem to flow together and your eye moves over the lines like water moving past her hull. It's different for each boat but they all have it, and it is one of the many subtle aspects of building a boat that shouldn't be missed by rushing.

In **Figure 1-4** Little Princess has been painted and her decks varnished; she's sitting in the water, waiting. Forty hours is a reasonable amount of time to spend on finish and painting; more than that I consider just a waste of time. Time you could be using your boat.

Actually, I spend approximately twenty hours on finishing a boat the size of Little Princess. My attitude is, boats are not works of art; they are meant to be in the water, and if they are in the water they will get bumped and scraped.

If you have spent hours lovingly finishing out your boat to a flawless finish, each bump and scrape will be incredibly painful. It will be so painful that you will stop using your boat.

I've seen it happen more than once. There are at least two of my canoes hanging on walls because the owners thought they were too pretty to use. So don't worry about building a flawless boat, just do a good job and enjoy your boat in the water . . . where it's supposed to be.

Figure 1-4

2

The Stuff Boats Are Made Of

Plywood is the main component of all the boats in this book. The bulkheads, the planking, and the decks are all made with plywood. Not just any plywood; these boats are built with marine plywood. And not just marine plywood, but marine plywood manufactured to British Standard 1088.

So what is BS1088 marine plywood and what makes it preferable to other plywoods? Plywood manufactured to BS1088 standards must meet a long list of requirements about glue type, veneer thickness, voids (the absence of voids, really), and the absence of splits or breaks in the veneers; all the wood in the veneers must have a specified resistance to fungus (rot). Really, it's far more complex than this very general overview, but what it boils down to is, BS1088 plywood is the best plywood for constructing your boat.

This means all plywood that has the BS1088 stamp is exactly the same, right? Unfortunately, it's not that simple. I have found considerable variation in plywood with the BS1088 label. This seems to be the experience of other boatbuilders as well.

The most obvious is the appearance of the surface veneers. In some cases the surface veneer just wasn't very pretty. While this might not mean

much for boat that is meant to be painted, it is significant for the boat meant to be varnished. I don't think this has an effect on the longevity of the plywood, but it is something to consider.

Another area where I have seen some difference is with the interior veneers. The more expensive brands have more consistent interior veneers. The interior veneers are the same species as the surface veneers and the same quality.

If there is so much variation within plywood with the BS1088 standard, how can you be sure to get good-quality plywood? The answer is to order plywood with a Lloyds of London certification. This is your guarantee, so to speak, that the manufacturer has complied with all the 1088 standards and not just the minimum standards.

Due to the more stringent standards, plywood that carries the Lloyds certification is more expensive than the other plywood, but it's worth the extra expense. **Figure 2-1** shows Okoume plywood with the Lloyds stamp. The stamp is important, particularly if you are ordering long distance and paying shipping costs in addition to the plywood. Certainly the last thing you want, when you pop open the crate, is to be disappointed.

Figure 2-1

If you are fortunate enough to have a lumberyard close at hand that carries BS1088 ply, you can look before you buy and see if there is a big quality drop. Another alternative is ordering from an established supplier, like long time advertisers in *WoodenBoat* magazine, *Messing About In Boats*, or *Boatbuilder* magazine. This will lessen your chances of being disappointed by the quality of the plywood you ordered. Also, when I order long distance, I like to speak to a salesperson rather than order online. That way I can explain my needs and he or she can describe their products in detail.

There is one more item in the whole marine plywood/BS1088 plywood lumber pile that can cause some confusion. In addition to BS1088 plywood, there is another plywood that carries the British Standard 6555 stamp. There are those who will try to tell you that BS6555 is the same or just as good as BS1088, but this is just not so. BS6555 requirements are not as stringent as the BS1088 standards. I was told several years ago by a supplier that plywood with the BS6555 stamp is exterior-grade plywood but not marine grade.

Can you use BS6555 plywood in your boat? Yes, I've built several boats using BS6555. Just be aware that it's not the same as BS1088 plywood. You will find an occasional void in the core veneers, and the thickness of the interior veneers will not be as consistent as in BS1088 plywood. In other words, it is inferior-quality plywood, and this is why it is less expensive.

All of this plywood, whether it's BS1088 or BS6555, is measured in millimeters, not inches. If you try to order plywood using inches it will get confusing, so learn to order in millimeters. It's really easy if you remember that 3mm plywood is almost exactly 1/8 inch thick, 4mm plywood is almost exactly 5/32 inch thick and 6mm plywood is almost exactly ¼ inch thick.

That's pretty straightforward because a 3mm sheet is 3mm, a 4mm sheet is 4mm and so on, but some sheets will be 48 inches by 96 inches (4 feet by 8 feet) and others will be 48 1/16 inches by 98 7/16 inches or 2500mm x 1220mm. This doesn't make any difference and sometimes the extra 2½ inches can mean you only have to make one scarf instead of two. However, it will be safe to assume that all the plywood will be at least 48 x 96; if you get the extra 2 ½ inches, that's just a bonus.

Almost all the boat is made with plywood but there is a small portion made from solid lumber. There is some trim on these boats, and the choice of that wood is really an aesthetic one. In the past I have used mahogany almost exclusively for trim; when I didn't use mahogany, I used cherry. Both these woods are now hard to find, and I've shifted to fir for the trim. I like the color of fir, it comes in long lengths, and it can have a very nice grain pattern, which is always a plus.

Occasionally I have used lyptus and Spanish cedar and I like these as well. Both lyptus and Spanish cedar are plantation-grown woods, and I like using plantation-grown woods when I can. I think plantation-grown trees are more ecologically sound, but I'm sure there are some who would disagree with that statement.

Whatever your feelings, both have nice color and take varnish well, but they can be hard to find locally. Generally, if you want to keep things simple, just use fir for the trim. It will look great varnished.

The trim on all these boats, regardless of the type of wood, is mechanically fastened. This means that the trim is held in place with screws. It's also held in place with epoxy, but the screws are used to hold it while the epoxy cures and then left in place. Because the screws are left in place, you will want to use either stainless steel or silicone bronze screws.

At one point, I only used silicone bronze screws because bronze doesn't rust, it is nonmagnetic and it's very traditional. I was fairly dogmatic about it, but after I twisted off a fair number of bronze screws and stripped out the driver slot of a bunch, I began to doubt the wisdom of my choice. This all occurred because bronze is soft, and when the clutch of the driver is set too high, one of the above will happen.

I decided that stainless steel, which doesn't rust, is nonmagnetic and is much harder than bronze, might be better choice. When I first switched to stainless screws I felt that I was somehow violating tradition, but that has passed. At this point I've built a number of boats with stainless-steel screws and will probably not use bronze screws again because I'm happy with the results.

The choice of screws and type of trim will, more than likely, be made on availability. There is positively nothing wrong with making a choice based on that; I do it all the time. However, you should buy the best-quality products you can. You'll never find yourself saying, "I wish I had used cheaper stuff to build the boat," but you might find yourself saying, "I wish I used better stuff to build the boat."

Materials Lists for the Canoes

Little Princess (12 feet) and Lutra One (14 feet)

1 4 x 8 sheet of 6mm plywood—bottom
4 4 x 8 sheets of 4mm plywood—planks and bulkheads
1 4 x 8 sheet of 3mm plywood—decks

40 to 45 lineal feet of 5/8 x 3/4 basswood, poplar, or fir for the sheer clamps and cleats
40 to 45 lineal feet of 5/8 x 3/4 cherry, mahogany, or fir for the inwales and outwales

A 4-foot-long 2 x 12 piece of cherry, mahogany, fir or pine will be needed for the false stem. Depending on the layout, a piece less than 12 inches wide can be used. The cherry and mahogany will probably come in 4/4, 6/4, or 8/4. 4/4 should work if surfaced to 15/16 plus or minus.

8/4 would be overkill and have to be surfaced down. The yard should be able to surface the plank for a charge if you don't have a planer.

1.5 to 2 gallons of epoxy resin plus appropriate hardener
2 5-quart containers of thickening agent Cab-O-Sil (silica)
1 quart wood flour
1 box of 100 #6 x 3/4 bronze or stainless-steel wood screws
1 box of 100 #6 x 5/8 bronze or stainless-steel wood screws

1 roll (50 yards) 3-inch 4- or 6-ounce fiberglass tape
5 yards of 50-inch-wide 4-ounce fiberglass cloth (use 6-ounce for heavy abrasion)

Disposable rubber gloves
Disposable brushes
Measuring cups for epoxy
Stirring sticks
1 box of 1- to 1½-inch fine finish nails or brads
Rags or paper towels for wiping up excess epoxy

2 sheets 5/8-inch or 3/4-inch particleboard or MDF for molds. (Rip sheets into 24 x 96 pieces if the baseline is to be 24 inches above the strongback, or (say) 16 x 96 if the baseline is to be 16 inches Twenty-four inches will be best.) Each blank should be cut just slightly wider than the maximum beam at that station. Also, you need masking or plastic tape for the edges of the molds. **Be sure to tape the edges of all the molds or they will become a permanent but unwanted part of the boat!**

1 sheet of 3/4-inch plywood for the strongback, ripped into 6-inch-wide strips.

Lutra Two (16 feet)

5 4 x 8 sheets of 4mm plywood—planks and bulkheads

1 4 x 8 sheet of 3mm plywood—decks

1 4 x 8 sheet of 6mm—bottom

40 to 45 lineal feet of 5/8 x ¾ basswood, poplar, or fir for the sheer clamps and cleats

40 to 45 lineal feet of 5/8 x ¾ cherry, mahogany, or fir for the inwales and outwales

A 4-foot-long 2 x 12 piece of cherry, mahogany, fir or pine will be needed for the false stem. Depending on the layout, a piece less than 12 inches wide can be used. The cherry and mahogany will probably come in 4/4, 6/4, or 8/4. 4/4 should work if surfaced to 15/16 plus or minus. 8/4 would be overkill and have to be surfaced down. The yard should be able to surface the plank for a charge if you don't have a planer.

1.5 to 2 gallons of epoxy resin plus hardener

2 5-quart containers of thickening agent Cab-O-Sil (silica)

1 quart wood flour

1 box of 100 #6 x ¾ bronze or stainless-steel wood screws

1 box of 100 #6 x 5/8 bronze or stainless-steel wood screws

1 roll (50 yards) 3-inch 4- or 6-ounce fiberglass tape

6 yards of 50-inch-wide 4-ounce fiberglass cloth (use 6-ounce for heavy abrasion)

Disposable rubber gloves

Disposable brushes

Measuring cups for epoxy

Stirring sticks

1 box of 1- to 1½ inch fine finish nails or brads

Rags or paper towels for wiping up excess epoxy

2 sheets 5/8-inch or ¾-inch particleboard or MDF for molds. (Rip sheets into 24 x 96 pieces if the baseline is to be 24 inches above the strongback or (say) 16 x 96 if the baseline is to be 16 inches above the strongback. Twenty-four inches will be best.) Each blank should be cut just slightly wider than the maximum beam at that station. Also, you need masking or plastic tape for the edges of the molds. **Be sure to tape the edges of all the molds or they will become a permanent but unwanted part of the boat!**

1 sheet of ¾-inch plywood for the strongback, ripped into 6-inch-wide strips.

3

The Glue That Binds

The boats in this book are built using epoxy. In fact there aren't many screws or mechanical fasteners used. What holds these boats together is epoxy, just epoxy. But epoxy does more than hold everything together; it waterproofs the wood as well. That's almost as important, because keeping water out of the wood prevents the wood from rotting.

Because both these jobs are very important and probably nothing is more important than holding your boat together, you want to use a good-quality marine epoxy. There are at least three major brands of marine epoxies: System Three, MAS, and West System. All are good, and I have used all three.

West System epoxy, which has been on the market since 1971, uses a 5:1 mixing ratio—that is, 5 parts resin to 1 part hardener. West System is a good epoxy and in some people's minds is almost synonymous with epoxy.

I've used West System and it has always performed like I've wanted and expected. What I don't like is the 5:1 ratio. I personally find this a bother and believe that a 5:1 ratio is not as forgiving of mistakes as a 2:1 ratio. The nice people at West System would, I suspect, disagree with me, and I want to state, up front, that the above is a personal opinion —nothing more. There are many boatbuilders who swear by West System and would be highly offended if you would suggest they use something else.

I used MAS epoxy for the first time when I taught a class at WoodenBoat School in 2005. Because I had no previous experience with MAS I ran a series of tests to get a feel for pot life, how long it takes for the epoxy to cure, and to calibrate the measuring pumps. My students built seven boats with it, and the epoxy did its job well. It always performed as expected; there was never a failure of a batch to cure. This is important because a failed batch of epoxy can be an inconvenience at best and a disaster in the worst case. It's just something you never want to happen. My experience with MAS is limited to that class, and there was nothing negative about the experience.

That leaves System Three. I have used it for over 15 years and I have built every boat in my shop with System Three resins. During those 15 years I never felt the need or desire to change epoxy brands. It always worked and worked well.

There are some reasons why I've used System Three continuously for 15 years. First, System Three uses a 2:1 mixing ratio, 2 parts resin to 1 part hardener. This is simple and straightforward and probably more forgiving of small errors in mixing. Let me say, right now, that no epoxy is forgiving of large errors in mixing. Therefore, great care needs to be taken when mixing. And, for my brain, it's easier to take care when the mixing ratio is 2 resin to 1 hardener.

That 2:1 ratio has another benefit for mixing small batches of resin: Small batches of resin are important because it means less waste. All the cured epoxy sitting in the bottom of mixing cups is wasted epoxy and wasted money. There will be many times that you will want just a very small amount of epoxy, and I can mix 1 ounce of resin and ½ ounce of hardener very easily. You have to be careful, but it's something I do all the time. Also, little batches aren't necessarily just for little boats. I have built some fairly big boats using small batches of epoxy because it means less waste.

The second reason I like System Three general purpose resin is that I find it's more resistant to "amine blush" than either West System or MAS. Just what is "amine blush"? It's a slick, greasy film that forms on the surface of the epoxy as it cures. You can wash it off with water but it's just better not to have to deal with it. If you don't wash it off the next layer won't adhere and you've got a problem. Actually, according to System Three, their SilverTip Laminating Resin, which I now use, doesn't blush at all. I have certainly found this to be the case during the construction of six boats.

So I recommend System Three epoxies and SilverTip Laminating Resin in particular. Building a boat involves a commitment of time and effort; buy the best epoxy you can afford and then measure and mix it carefully.

Virtually all the failures of epoxy to cure—that's right, virtually all failures—can be traced to problems with either or both. Epoxy doesn't have much latitude with measuring or mixing. That's true for all epoxies, not just System Three.

Over the fifteen or so years I've been building and designing boats, I developed a few tricks for measuring and mixing epoxy. Mixing—that is, the stirring together of resin and hardener—is very straightforward; a small batch, 1½ to 3 ounces, is mixed at least 60 seconds by the clock, and batches 3 to 9 ounces are mixed 90 to 120 seconds by the clock. Even after 15 years I still glance at my watch to be sure I mix long enough. It may seem silly, but just do it; you won't be sorry. Batches over 9 ounces should increase mixing times according to the size of the batch, but I rarely mix a batch over 9 ounces—it just wastes too much epoxy.

Measuring epoxy is much less straightforward because there are several ways to do the job. Actually, there are more than several but I'm only going to talk about measuring by volume because that's what I find to be the easiest.

The most basic is the 1-ounce cup (**Figure 3-1**). These little cups are inexpensive and can be reused with minimal care. Just wipe them out after each use and don't mix the resin cups with the hardener cups. I have built a good many boats using nothing but 1-ounce cups to measure the epoxy, and I always have a package of 100 around my shop for odd measuring jobs.

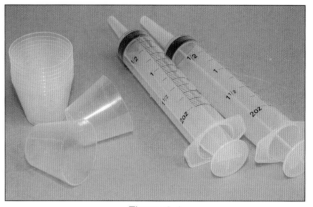

Figure 3-1

Also in **Figure 3-1** are graduated syringes, which are almost as simple as the 1-ounce cups. The syringes also require that you clean them after each use and not mix the hardener syringe with the resin syringe. Mixing them up will cause the epoxy to cure in the syringe, and they will have to be replaced. This can be avoided by putting red paint or tape on the hardener syringe and blue or black paint/tape on the resin syringe. A Magic Marker will wash off and confusion will be the result, so use paint or tape.

The next level up from syringes and cups is what is commonly referred to as the mustard pump. That's because basically it is the same pump used to dispense mustard and catsup. One pump sits in the resin container and one sits in the hardener container. Some are calibrated to deliver 2 units of resin with a single stroke and 1 unit of hardener with a single stroke; others deliver equal amounts. If they are not calibrated and each delivers an equal amount then take even greater care in counting the strokes. If the ratio is 2:1 then you will have to pump 10 resins and then 5 hardeners. This isn't impossible, but it leaves more room for error. So if you are going to use pumps, calibrated pumps will be best.

There is a downside to the mustard pumps—they are not always accurate. When my students used the pumps at WoodenBoat School, I checked the calibration every morning and then again at lunch. The little 1-ounce cups are perfect for this. If you use the pumps, it will be very important to do the same. This will be particularly true if there is a long time between uses. Conversations with other boatbuilders seem to indicate that the pumps will lose their prime over a day or so of disuse, and the first one or two strokes will not be the full amount. This was not a problem I experienced, but then the pumps were in constant use.

One thing I do like about the pumps is their ability to measure small batches; of course, this is the same thing I like about the other two methods. And while small batches of epoxy help cut down on waste, mistakes in measuring will create not only waste but perhaps big problems. I learned this the hard way so I developed a rule about measuring very quickly: **Don't do anything else when measuring, just measure.** Unless you use a pump that automatically measures both resin and hardener with one stroke (these are very expensive) you will be counting ounces of resin and ounces of hardener. And it's very easy to lose count.

Let me relate an experience I've had more than once. I would start to mix 6 ounces of resin and 3 ounces of hardener in a cup. I would get to 5 ounces of resin in the cup and the phone would ring, someone would come in the shop, or any number of other distractions would occur. When I returned, I was never sure exactly how much resin was in the cup, so rather than guess and be wrong I poured the resin out. It couldn't go back into the big jug of resin because it might contaminate the entire jug.

At some point I found a better way. **Figure 3-2** shows how I mix 6 ounces of resin and 3 ounces of hardener. All the resin or hardener is put in each

Figure 3-2

individual cup before any is poured into the mixing cup. Then, if there is an interruption, I can come back to see what has been poured and what has not. There is no question because it's all right there. This isn't foolproof, of course, but it almost is.

The pumps are a little harder to make foolproof. When I'm teaching a class I do have a hard-and-fast rule that there is to be no talking at the pumps. That allows everyone to focus on counting and nothing else. This has minimized mistakes; only a batch or two has had to be discarded.

I suppose you could use a tick stick or keep tally marks for every five pumps, but that may be more of a distraction. Something similar could be devised for the syringes, but the main thing is to have a system and stick to it. Do it the same each and every time. Be rigid and meticulous about measuring and you will never be sorry. Be lax or careless and, well . . .

There is one pump that does allow for a more relaxed attitude, but it is expensive; the builder of one or two boats, even three or four, would find it hard to justify the cost (**Figure 3-3**). However, even this pump can lose accuracy if the epoxy is too cold. The light warms the epoxy and keeps the pump consistent. You will find that a light will be of benefit with any of the measuring systems in cool or cold weather. As the temperature drops, the epoxy will become more and more viscous (thicker), and that's why the pumps have problems.

Even fairly viscous epoxy will flow downhill, so if you want it to stay in one place, such as a bulk-

Figure 3-3

head, it will have to have a thickener added. There are several but the one I like best is silica thickener or Cab-O-Sil. Cab-O-Sil and silica thickener are basically the same, by the way, but Cab-O-Sil is a trade name like Coke or Kleenex. Add this to the epoxy after the hardener has been thoroughly mixed in and it creates a non-sagging, gap-filling adhesive. (Note: Silica thickener or Cab-O-Sil is light, fluffy, easily airborne and definitely not good to breathe; wear a dust mask when using.)

You will find that I describe how thick the epoxy should be by comparing it to heavy cream, catsup, mayonnaise, peanut butter, and crunchy peanut butter. I like to use these comparisons because everybody knows about how thick any of these are. What happens if your mayonnaise is not as thick as or is thicker than my epoxy mayonnaise? Absolutely nothing; these are meant as a way to qualify a very subjective description, like *fairly thick* or *kind of runny* and I just like saying, "Mix me up a batch of crunchy peanut butter epoxy."

Actually, when you add wood flour (another thickening agent) to the silica-thickened epoxy it does look like crunchy peanut butter. Which is probably why I started using food items to describe how thick to make the epoxy.

Even though wood flour is a thickening agent or a thixotropic agent, I use it to just color the thick-

ened epoxy. Cab-O-Sil or silica thickener is white, really white, and does not look good next to varnished wood, so I color the epoxy with wood flour until it matches the wood. This isn't hard; just add a pinch at a time until the right color is achieved. It's kind of like kindergarten when you got to play with finger paints. **Figure 3-4** shows epoxy thickened with silica only (left) and the same batch with wood flour added (right). I think it would be good to point out that I have always had trouble with glue joints where wood flour has been used as the only thickener, so I use it just as a coloring agent.

Figure 3-4

Wood flour, by the way, is a specific product. It really looks like flour and not like sawdust. I made that mistake once when I mixed sawdust in the epoxy. The result was not pleasant to look at, and it was not smooth at all. Fortunately, I had the presence of mind to scrape it off the boat before it hardened. So use Cab-O-Sil to thicken epoxy, wood flour to color it, and never use sawdust thinking it will be just as good and save a little money.

Of course, there's nothing wrong with saving money, but cutting corners with the quality of the epoxy is not a place to do so. Invest in the best epoxy you can afford. If it's one of the three brands listed here, you can't go wrong.

4

Reading the Plans

Plans are a convenient way to describe, in great detail, a specific boat. Even with a simple canoe like Little Princess there is a large amount of information in the plans—but you have to be able to understand the plans to extract any details. While that may seem so obvious it's hardly worth stating, understanding all the information on a set of plans can be somewhat intimidating.

I know because I've been intimidated by a set of boat plans. Years ago, my desire to build a boat reached critical mass when I discovered a lovely little sailboat. It was beautiful and I had fallen in love. I couldn't wait to get started so I paid extra to have my first set of plans rushed to me.

When the plans arrived I dropped what I was doing, tore open the envelope, and spread five sheets out on the table. There wasn't a manual or any notes of explanation, just those five bewildering pages of plans. Bewilderment slowly became outrage. I was outraged that anyone would expect me to build a boat from those sheets of paper.

Of course, there was more than enough information there to build a boat; I just couldn't understand it. Let me assume that you are standing where I stood years ago, and before bewilderment turns into outrage, help you understand that information.

For many people the table of offsets, which is found on the plans sheet in the appendix, is the

most bewildering because it seems to be a jumble of numbers. However, it's very easy once you understand that it's simply the key to an X-Y axis graph. The X axis represents half the width of the boat, also called a half breadth, and the Y axis represents the height of the boat. **Figure 4-1** shows how the information in the table of offsets relates to an X-Y axis graph. Each unit on the graph is equal to 1 foot, and that unit is broken down into 12 inches, and that unit is broken down into 8 fractions of an inch. **Figure 4-1** locates a point that is 7 3/8 inches up on the Y axis and 11 3/8 inches over on the X axis.

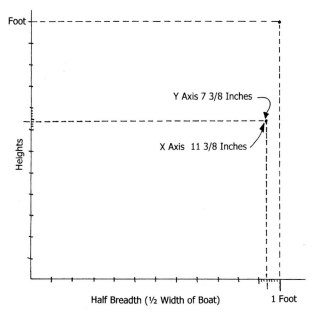

Figure 4-1

There's nothing complicated about that, but what can be confusing is the way information is written down. Measurements are written in feet, inches, and eighths of an inch. For example, 1 foot 6¾ inches, would be written in the table of offsets as 1-6-6. So ¾ of an inch is left 6/8 inch instead of being reduced to ¾. Just remember, the last place is for eighths of an inch. So the measurements in **Figure 4-1** would be expressed as 0 feet 7 inches 3 eights or 0-7-3 and the measurements for the X axis would be written 0 feet 11 inches and 3 eights or 0-11-3. It may take a little while to become

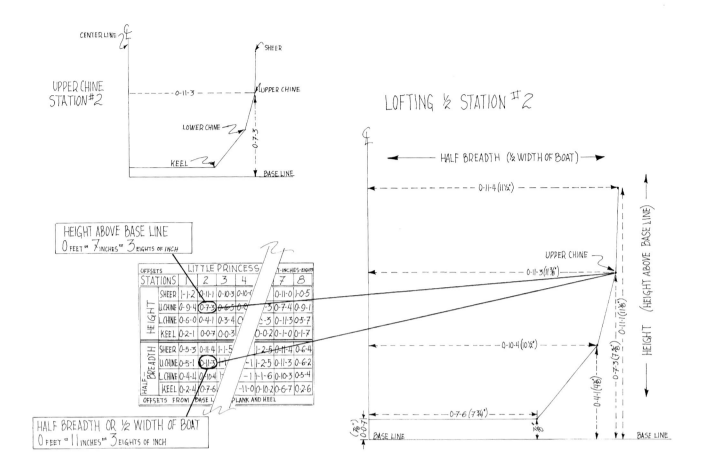

Figure 4-2

accustomed to that, particularly when dealing with 4 eighths and 6 eighths, because all of us were taught to reduce fractions. However, it's easier when you transfer the information to the graph.

There are some other terms on the table of offsets that can be somewhat confusing as well. If you look at the partial table of offsets in **Figure 4-2** you'll notice that the table is divided into half breadths and heights, which is the X axis and the Y axis, and then both of those are divided into keel, l. chine (lower chine), u. chine (upper chine), and sheer.

The keel, l. chine (lower chine), u. chine (upper chine), and sheer are specific names for points on the boat and correspond to specific points on the X-Y axis graph. Look just above the table of offsets in **Figure** 4-2 and you'll see where each of the points falls on the boat, or rather a cross section of the boat.

Now look just to the right of the table of offsets

and you can see the half breadth and height measurements for each of those points and where each measurement came from in the table of offsets. The half breadth and height of the upper chine are circled in the table, but it's easy to see where each measurement came from and how it corresponds to each place-name.

This information tells you how to locate the keel and the chines on the X-Y axis graph, but these groups of points are also bundled into stations. **Figure** 4-3 shows how the stations place the half breadths and heights that determine the shape of the boat. It's not very difficult to imagine each station as a slice of the boat just like the slice of a loaf of bread. Station #2 is a slice that is a particular distance from the very front of the boat. In fact slices/Stations #1 through #8 are all at specific distances from the very front of the boat.

Occasionally the specific distances for the sta-

21

Figure 4-3

tions will be listed somewhere in the table of off-sets. This will most likely be the case if the spacing is an equal distance for the length of the boat. You'll find it listed as "station spacing 24 inches," or "station spacing 3 feet," indicating that each station or slice is 24 inches apart, 3 feet apart, or whatever the spacing might be, for the length of the boat.

I like to list the spacing for each station separately because many times the spacing is not equal. In this book you'll find the distance for each station just under the table of offsets, which is in the appendix.

Another piece of information that will aid in visualizing how to put this boat together is: the baseline is not the same as the strongback. In fact,

they are opposite each other and the baseline is 24 inches above the strongback (**Figure 4-4**).

Why 24 inches? I have found that this allows easy access to the underside of the boat and still allows the bottom to be reached without undue effort when the strongback is sitting on sawhorses.

All of the above information wasn't there with that original set of plans; it was assumed I had enough knowledge to read and understand what was there. I didn't, of course, but what I have tried to do here is give you enough knowledge to get started. I think you'll find, as I did, that each piece of knowledge builds on the other, and the process becomes clearer as you proceed.

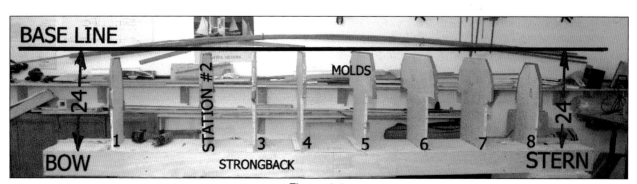

Figure 4-4

5

Lofting Station #2

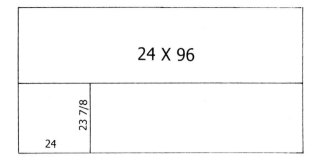

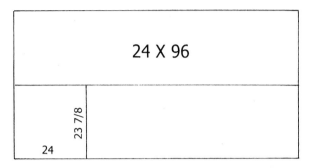

Figure 5-1

There really isn't anything hard about lofting. It is, after all, just an X-Y axis graph, and there is nothing mysterious about that. Also the process of lofting one station mold is the same for every other station so we'll loft Station #2 because we've already talked about it.

The first task is to decide on the type of material you will use for the station molds. I like to use ¾-inch MDF or particleboard. Either of these cheap, but heavy, materials will do very nicely. Particleboard is slightly cheaper, I believe, and that makes it my first choice. You can use ¾-inch plywood, but this will certainly be more expensive. I don't recommend C-D pine plywood because there are too many voids; in my experience, it doesn't make good mold material. You'll need two 4 x 8 sheets of whichever material you choose to buy.

Figure 5-1 diagrams how to rip the two sheets of MDF. Cutting a 24-inch by 96-inch piece will leave the drop 23 7/8 inches by 96 inches. I've tried to split the sheet so the saw kerf leaves two pieces 23 15/16 inches but it rarely works, so just rip the sheet at 24 inches. The drop doesn't go to waste; as you can see in the drawing, you cut two or more pieces 24 inches by 23 7/8 inches for blanks. You'll want be as accurate as possible at this point.

It's not a problem if you don't have a way to rip a 4 x 8 sheet of plywood, because most lumber-yards will make the cuts for you. I've found that many yards, particularly the large building supply stores, will have a panel saw designed to cut 4 x 8 sheets accurately. You'll probably be charged a cutting fee, but this will be money well spent.

The next step is to take those as-accurate-as-possible 24-inch by 96-inch pieces and cut them into blanks for each mold. This will mean finding what the maximum half breadth is for each station, which is at the sheer, and doubling that number. In the case of Station #2 the half breadth at the sheer is 0-11-4 or 0 feet 11 inches and 4 eights. Doubled that's 23 inches, but you'll want to add about an inch and cut it at 24 by 24 inches. The extra space allows for a more accurate cut at the sheer.

Figure 5-2 shows the blank for Station #2 with the centerline drawn; both the baseline and strongback sides have been labeled as well. Labeling both the baseline and strongback gives an important visual reference. I've lofted many boats and I still label the baseline, because it reduces the chances for mistakes. It's a constant reminder that all the measurements are taken **up** from the baseline and **over** from the centerline.

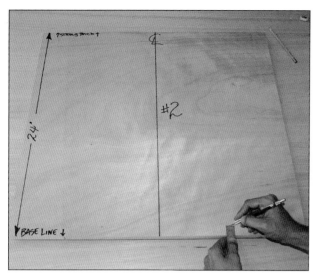

Figure 5-2

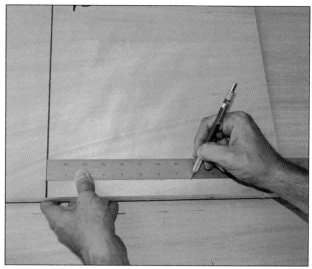

Figure 5-3

I think you'll find starting with the keel (the bottom of the boat) is the most logical progression; it's certainly the way I prefer to loft. Checking the table of offsets (see the plans on page 156) shows that the height of the keel at Station #2 is 0-0-7 or 0 feet, 07/8 inch above the baseline (the bottom edge of the mold). So measure up from the bottom edge of the blank/mold 7/8 inch and place a pencil mark. (I like to use a pencil because mistakes are easily erased.) Move over to the centerline and place another pencil mark 7/8 inch up from the bottom edge of the mold/baseline, then move to the left of the centerline about 6 to 8 inches, measure up 7/8 inch, and put another pencil mark.

Now go back to the table of offsets and you'll find that the keel half breadth (one half the width of the boat at the keel) for Station #2 is 0-7-6 or 0 feet, 7 6/8 inches. Then, just like in **Figure 5-3**, place your ruler on those marks you made 7/8 inch up from the baseline (this keeps the ruler parallel to the baseline) and measure over 7 6/8 inches from the centerline. This point is 7/8 inch up from the baseline (the height of the keel at Station #2) and 7 6/8 inches over from the centerline; mark this point with a dark dot. This is half the keel at Station #2, so you'll want to repeat the process for the other half

and then draw a line connecting the two dots (**Figure 5-4**). Now measure the full width of the keel to be sure it is exactly twice 7 6/8 inches (15 4/8 inches). If it's not exactly 15½ inches or exactly 7/8 of an inch above the baseline (bottom edge of the blank), then there is a mistake and now is the time to correct it.

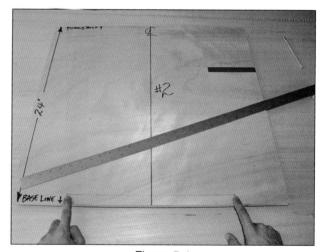

Figure 5-4

Be sure to check each measurement for the full width and height; make sure it is correct and then move to next set of points. It's a good habit to check and double-check each measurement. If you learn to move slowly and methodically as you loft each point, you can catch mistakes before they create problems.

Figure 5-13

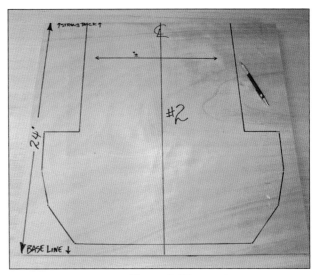

Figure 5-15

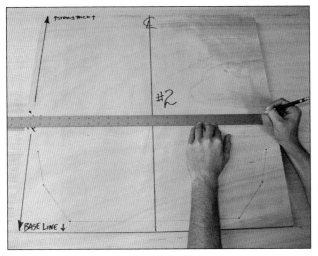

Figure 5-14

Go to the table of offsets and locate the height for the sheer at Station #2 (0-11-1 or 11 1/8 inches above the baseline); mark the centerline as before (**Figure 5-13**). Again, put a light mark at 11 1/8 inches above the baseline on each side of the centerline and—using those marks to keep the ruler parallel to the baseline—mark the half breadth of the sheer (0-11-3 or 11 3/8 inches) as in **Figure 5-14**. Just as you did for the lower chine and upper chine, check everything and then connect the sheer to upper chine.

With the sheer lofted you have basically finished Station #2; however, there are a few more steps left. **Figure 5-15** illustrates how I like to finish each sta-

tion mold. The strongback will be 16 inches wide, and I find having the mold 16 inches wide where it attaches at the strongback works very well. This gives plenty of width for the mold to attach to the cleat on the strongback.

Just put some marks 8 inches on either side of the centerline and strike a line from sheer to sheer. Now bring the lines on either side of the centerline up until they intersect the line connecting the two sheer points. Make these dark so they will be easy to see.

There are a couple of molds where the maximum beam is less than 16 inches. In that case draw your line across from sheer point to sheer point just like on #2 and then drop a line down that is inside the maximum beam.

The last task is to transfer the centerline on the mold to the other side. This is important when you put the molds on the strongback because you want to see the centerline on both sides. I like to use a small square to draw the line on the top and bottom of the mold. I think this is the most accurate way to make the transfer. Also, you will find this easier if the job is done before you cut out the molds.

Now that you've lofted a station mold, the process is the same for each of the eight molds. I do want to make it very clear that I have given you just enough information to loft the molds for the three boats in this book, nothing more. There are a large number of books that have been written just about lofting, and they are worth reading if you want to know more. Classes are also taught on how to loft a boat. I would certainly encourage you take a class or read several books—it will be worth the effort.

Also, I choose to loft each mold separately rather than loft all the stations on a sheet of paper and then transfer than information to the mold material. I've used that method, but lofting each mold individually works best for me.

You'll find as you build these boats that there are several ways to accomplish the same task. Is one better than another? Is there a right way to build a boat? The answer is no. I've always said that if you have 10 different boatbuilders working side by side, each building the same boat, you'll see ten different ways to build that boat. In fact, it has been pointed out to me by several of my fellow builders that what you would see are twenty ways to build that boat because each of us knows at least two perfectly good ways to accomplish the same task.

So if you have another way to loft or you think of a way that will work better for you I encourage you to use that method. If not the way detailed above has worked for me and it will work for you. The most important things to remember are to work carefully, be methodical, check your work, and then recheck your work.

I think one other lesson I learned might be beneficial at this juncture. I tend to be very goal oriented, and building a boat is a long-term goal. I learned to take pleasure and find achievement in each task. I learned to look at lofting a single station, like Station #2, as an achievement—as a goal accomplished. At the end of the day I could see that lofted station, not as symbol of how far I had to go to the finish, but as a goal reached. That lesson has served me well. I don't think I could have continued to build boats if I hadn't learned it.

As you loft each station and lean it against the wall, learn to see it as an individual achievement. This will add to the pleasure of building these boats.

6

Cutting Out the Station Molds and Bulkheads

The next step is to cut out all the station molds you have leaning against a wall. I like to cut right at the line but not cut the line out (**Figure 6-1**). Leaving the line gives a reference point and tells how accurate the cut is. If you weave way out from the line, a plane or belt sander can remove the extra material. If you weave way in, the break in the line tells you how much and how far the saw wandered. The main thing to remember is to take your time because it's hard to make big mistakes when the saber saw is moving slow. Also, if you put a fine-tooth plywood blade in the saber saw, you'll find the cut is much cleaner and has less tear-out.

Figure 6-1 shows station mold #2 being cut out. Station #2 and station #7 are important because there are bulkheads at those locations. The molds themselves will not be part of the boat. They will come out like the rest of the molds, but they will hold the bulkhead that does stay in the boat. So as they are cut, set them to one side and finish the rest of the station molds.

A bulkhead, by the way, is a wall that completely spans the hull. These bulkheads are watertight—the edges are sealed so water can't leak through—and they both have hatches to allow access into the compartment created by the bulkhead.

It's always easier to put in bulkheads during construction, so I like to have a station where a bulkhead falls. That way the bulkhead can just be nailed to the face of the station mold, and there is no time-consuming hand fitting once the boat is turned over.

Because the bulkhead is the same size as the station mold, all that is necessary is to trace its shape on a sheet of 4mm plywood approximately 28 inches by 16 inches (**Figure 6-2**) and cut it out. When you cut out the piece, don't cut right at the line but about 1/32 of an inch outside the line and then plane down to it (**Figure 6-3**). Cutting outside the line will keep the saw from cutting into the bulkhead. Remember to be careful, because this piece will be part of the boat.

Once the shape is cut and planed down, you'll need to lay out the centerline and the sheer line. The sheer line is particularly important because it

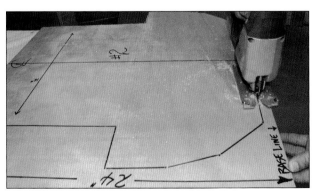
Figure 6-1

Figure 6-2

Figure 6-3

way that it is easy to stuff something through a hatch—but once it expands on the other side it can be almost impossible to get out. Also, the 7 3/8 x 15 size is about the maximum width and height you'll be able to fit into the bulkhead. It works well for me and I think it will work for you as well.

In **Figure 6-4** a 7 3/8 x 15 hatch has been laid out on the #2 bulkhead. All I did was measure up 1½ inches from the bottom of the bulkhead to establish the bottom line of the hatch. This gave me a line that was parallel to the bottom of the boat, and from that line I came up 7 3/8 inches for the top line of the hatch. Then I measured over 7½

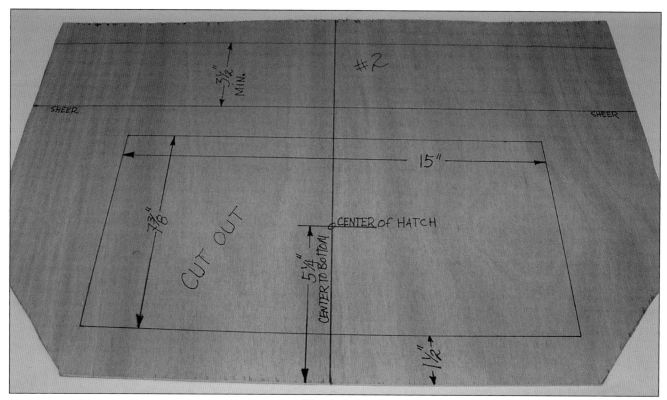

Figure 6-4

determines the maximum height of the hatch that will be in this bulkhead.

For me, one of the main criterion for establishing the hatch height and width was the diameter of the gear I wanted in the watertight storage areas. An inside dimension of 7 3/8 x 15 allowed for some fairly bulky items, like dry bags for clothes, to fit nicely and still be easy to remove. I learned the hard

inches (half of 15) for each side of the hatch, and that gave the inside dimensions on #2. The 3½ inches above the sheer line is for the deck camber or the convex shape of the deck.

The hatch in the bulkhead at Station #7 is a slightly different size, and **Figure 6-5** gives its layout. Using the line 1½ inches up from the bottom just like you did with #2 will give you the layout for

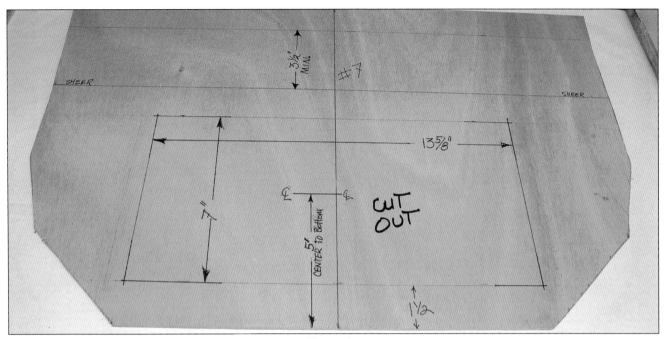

Figure 6-5

the hatch on #7. Notice that #7 also has at least 3½ inches above the sheer line for deck camber.

Once you have the layout drawn on #2 and #7, you'll want to epoxy a frame to the back side of each bulkhead. In **Figure 6-6**, ¾ x ¾ cleats have been placed just on the outside of the layout lines for the hatch and temporarily tacked in place with finish nails while the epoxy sets.

When the epoxy has set, cut out the material inside the frame. I use a router with a trim bit; this makes a fast and easy job of it. If you don't have a router, don't worry, because it's still an easy job.

Just use the saber saw to rough cut most of the

material out—but leave about ½ inch out from the frame. Now take the Japanese saw and cut out the rest using the frame as a guide.

At this point, just nail the bulkheads to their respective station molds and set them against the wall with the rest of the station molds. You'll want to be sure that the centerline of the bulkhead is matched up to the centerline on the station mold (**Figure 6-7**). Once you're satisfied that everything matches up, you can move on to the next step of lofting the stems.

Figure 6-6

Figure 6-7

Lofting the Stems

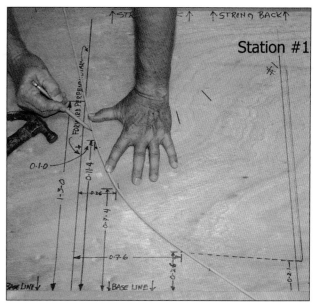

Figure 7-1

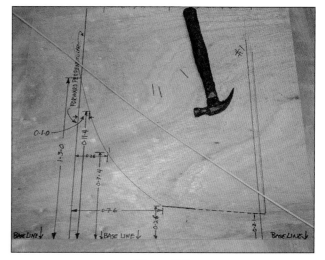

Figure 7-2

Lofting the stems really isn't that different from lofting the station molds. The points are still laid out on an X-Y axis graph, but they are connected by bending a thin batten rather than a straight edge.

The information you'll need to loft the stems for both the bow and the stern is found on either side of the table of offsets on the plans. (See page 156). Notice that the Y axis has become the forward perpendicular instead of the centerline, but the X axis is still the baseline. What is the forward perpendicular? It's the very front of the boat. The forward perpendicular is just a line that runs down perpendicular to the base from the forwardmost point of the boat.

In **Figure 7-1** the information on the plans has been reproduced full size on a piece of scrap plywood. And the baseline, strongback, and forward perpendicular have also been labeled. The distance from the baseline to the strongback is the same as the molds—24 inches. Also, Station #1 has been located 1-4-0 (1 foot, 4 0/8 inches) back from the FP (forward perpendicular) and 0-2-1 feet above the baseline. This information was taken from the table of offsets.

There are four points located on the curve of the stem: the heel of the stem where it joins the bottom, the lower chine, the upper chine, and the sheer. Those points are connected by a batten being

sprung so it touches all four. You'll want to use finish nails to hold the batten in place. I find 16 x 1½- or 2-inch finish nails work very well.

Once the batten is touching all the points, draw a line with a pencil. Be sure to hold the batten down with your hand so the line will reflect the true curve of the batten. **Figure 7-2** shows the batten removed and the fair line of the stem. However, what you see is the forwardmost edge of the stem; the rest of the stem needs to be drawn.

Figure 7-3 shows the finished shape of the stem. I like to make the distance from the front of the stem to the back edge about 1½ inches. I think this

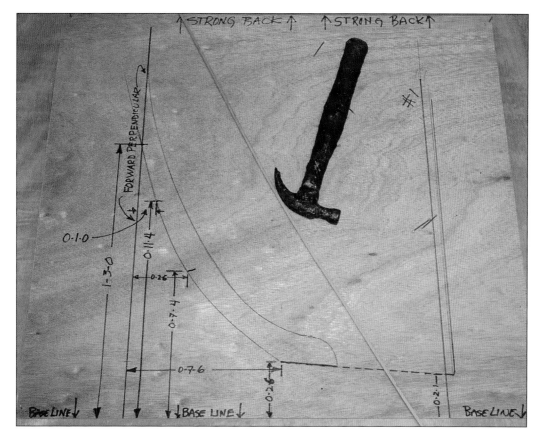

Figure 7-3

gives plenty of width without getting in the way. Notice the dotted line drawn from Station #1 to the point 0-7-6 back from the FP and up 0-2-6 from the baseline. This represents the line of the bottom and was needed so the shape of the stem would reflect that line. Also, the four points that determined the shape of the stem have been transferred to the cutout with tick marks.

Now all that is left to do is cut out this pattern (**Figure 7-4**) and use it to cut the stem that will go in the boat (**Figure 7-5**). I like to take 6mm scrap, laminate two pieces together, and cut the stem from the laminated piece.

The tick marks have been transferred from the pattern to stem as well. These tick marks are important because they represent where the garboard, mid-plank, and sheer plank will fall on the stem.

Just repeat the process for the stem at the stern and find a safe place to store these parts while you move on to the next task.

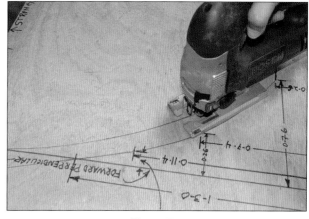

Figure 7-4

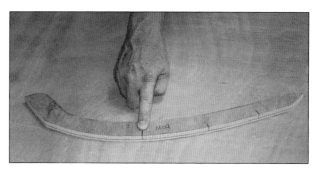

Figure 7-5

8

Scarfing

I've found that there are some boatbuilding tasks first time builders find very scary, and scarfing happens to be one of those tasks. If the truth be told, I found it scary as well. However, after cutting a great many scarfs, it's difficult to see what was so intimidating.

Briefly, scarfing is nothing more than joining two pieces of wood or plywood together to form a longer continuous plank or bigger piece of plywood. This generally involves cutting a matching slope on both pieces and then gluing them together with an adhesive such as epoxy (**Figure 8-1**).

The slope itself is expressed as a ratio like 8 to 1 (8:1) or 12 to 1 (12:1). For example, an 8:1 scarf in ¼-inch material would be 2 inches long; an 8:1 scarf in 4mm (5/32) material would be 1¼ inches long. It should be pointed out that an 8:1 scarf is the bare minimum and will require careful handling to keep the plank from breaking before it is attached to the boat. Actually, any scarfed plank

should be handled with care, turning so the scarf gets little or no stress, but an 8:1 scarf will require extra support on each side of the scarf as the plank is put on and taken off the molds. This kind of special care will lessen the chance of a snapped plank.

I prefer to use a 12:1 scarf as the minimum length, but will often use a scarf that is about 20:1 in thinner material. This means that a 12:1 scarf in ¼-inch or 6mm material should be 3 inches long. A 20:1 scarf in 4mm (5/32) is 31/8 inches long. I've found that a 20:1 slope is much less likely to have hard spots—spots that are stiffer than the rest of the plank—after glue-up.

And for glue-up it would be hard to find a better adhesive than epoxy, because the thickened epoxy can fill the small gaps where the slope doesn't match perfectly. This doesn't mean you can be careless and sloppy, but it does give a bit of latitude with the match. The closer the better, of course, and the perfectly cut slope is the goal.

The quest for the perfect slope has led to quite a few methods for scarfing plywood, and many involve some kind of shop-made jig. There is a jig for a router, a circle saw, and one jig I have heard about, but not seen, that involves turning a 4 x 8 sheet of plywood on edge and cutting the scarf on a table saw. Many of these shop-made jigs are detailed in various issues of *WoodenBoat* magazine and can be found there by those interested.

However, shop-made jigs can be too time consuming for the onetime builder, and most folks don't have a high enough ceiling in their shop to

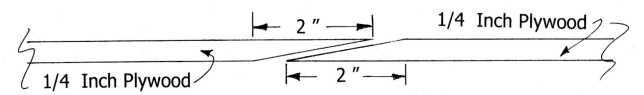

8:1 Scarf

Figure 8-1

upend a sheet of plywood. But all is not lost: There are several jigs you can buy, one method involves a tool you already have, and the last method doesn't use any tools.

The first jig you can buy requires a slight modification but otherwise is an out-of-the-box jig. **Figure 8-2** shows the two parts for this jig—a Bosch 1276 belt sander and its sanding frame, and the plywood base.

Figure 8-2

The plywood base is designed to capture the sander as it moves across the edge of the plywood being scarfed, and the aluminum sanding framing raises the sander at an angle to cut the scarf. Notice that the plywood base has two plywood guides in front and back of the sander/sanding frame. The front guide is permanent, but the back guide is removable to allow the marine plywood to be secured in the scarfing unit. To make reassembly easy, I've drawn a line where the removable guide is refastened each time; the other line is for the forward edge of the plywood. This line is 13½ inches from the face of the back/removable guide as indicated in the photo.

It will take a 60 x 48 base to scarf plywood 48 inches wide. The 60-inch width will allow enough

space on each side of the 48-inch-wide plywood for the sander frame. The base in **Figure 8-2** is 48 by 30 inches and I find this works very well; I seldom scarf a 48-inch-wide piece of plywood. Also, I only have about 1/8 inch play between the sanding frame and the two parallel guides. This seems to be about right for the frame to move easily back and forth without jamming.

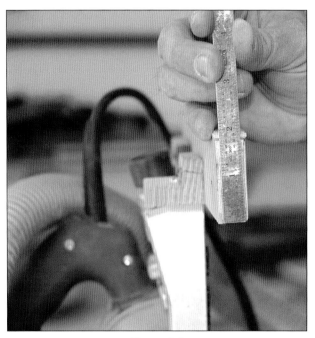

Figure 8-3

Figure 8-3 shows the only modification necessary to the frame. I've used two wooden L's to attach a ¾ x 2 x 15½ block to the back of the sanding frame. Another option is the small 90 degree corner braces, available at any building supply store, shown in **Figure 8-4**. Making the block about 15½ inches long seems to give enough bearing to control any twist in the sander/frame unit as it moves back and forth across the edge of the plywood.

A smooth back-and-forth motion is necessary because if the sander stops even for a moment, it will cut a gouge. I use a 40-grit belt on the sander, and it will cut a scarf in 4mm plywood in very short order.

Figure 8-4

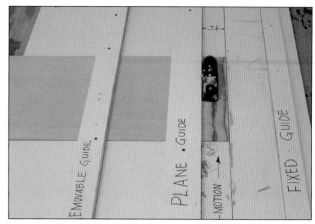

Figure 8-6

Figure 8-5

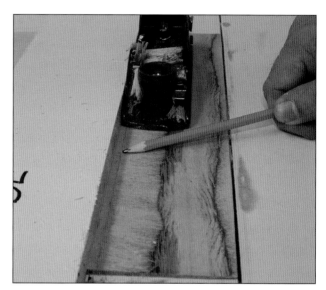

Figure 8-7

Figure 8-5 shows a scarf cut in 4mm plywood. Notice that the ply lines are fairly straight and parallel. This indicates that the slope is relatively even —that's something you will want to look for with any method you use. When I first started using this method, I would take a scarf like this and epoxy it together with its mate. It worked well, but I did find it was difficult to keep each board straight.

Because of this I included a couple more steps before glue-up. In **Figure 8-6** the sander has been removed and a guide screwed down 3 1/8 inches back from and parallel to the front edge of the plywood (a 20:1 scarf). Now put a block plane against the guide and plane down about 1/32 of an inch, maybe a little less. This creates a slight indention that the edge of the other sheet will rest in, and because the edge of both sheets is about 1/32 inch thick, it will be flush with the surface. This line is also a visual reference for aligning and keeping both sheets square during the glue-up process (**Figure 8-7**).

I've used this system for a number of years, and it has always worked very well. I keep the jig in a corner of my shop and bring it out when needed. However, in the beginning, with the addition of another accessory, I used the sander as an upright stationary sander. This helped because I didn't have an expensive tool sitting idle a good deal of the time.

One off-the-shelf scarfing unit may be the least expensive, particularly if you already have a 7 ½ inch circle saw. The 875 Scarfer, made and sold by West System epoxies, bolts directly on most circle saws. It requires that holes be drilled in the base so the two pieces of aluminum can be bolted on and removed easily. If you decide to purchase this unit, you will want to check with West System to be sure your circle saw is compatible with the unit.

I've used this scarfing attachment, and it does the job. Certainly for the builder who already has a circle saw, it is a good option. The attachment will allow plywood up to 3/8 inch thick to be scarfed with an 8:1 scarf. I find that the saw blade leaves a somewhat rough surface, but this is a minor issue. This is a small jig that can be stored in a drawer when off the circle saw, and that's a real plus in a very small space.

If you want to build the shop-made version of this jig, get *WoodenBoat* issue 175. Bill Thomas wrote a great article on how to construct both the jig and its integral hold-down system.

While the 875 Scarfer and the shop-made jig by Bill Thomas use a circle saw, the John Henry scarfer-planer uses a power plane. This unit has a rigid frame that screws to the bottom of a Makita 1900B 3 ¼ inch power planer; the larger unit screws to a Makita 1911B 4 3/8-inch power planer. The 1900B will scarf material up to 3/8 inch thick and is more than adequate for any of the boats in this book.

In addition to the rigid frame, this system also uses a base sheet much like the sander-scarfer uses. In **Figure 8-8** the base sheet has been temporarily fastened to the table and a piece of 4mm plywood tacked to the base sheet. **Figure 8-9** shows the planer with the guide runner (left side) pushed against the base sheet and positioned at the edge of the plywood to be scarfed. I've added a spacer to the guide runner and removed all the spaces from free side (right-side) runner.

Figure 8-8

Figure 8-9

Figure 8-10

Figure 8-11

Figure 8-13

The purpose of the spacers is to fine-tune the angle and depth of the cut. The base sheet needs to just touch the attachment plate for the depth of the cut to be correct (**Figure 8-10**). If the cut is too deep, you'll get an edge that looks like **Figure 8-11**.

I had to add an additional thin cardboard shim to get the depth of cut just right. The runner guide comes set for a 9mm base sheet, but I was using a 12mm base sheet. Because of that I added a spacer to the guide runner, but I still needed to add two more thin shims. Also, I pulled the spacer from the free-side (right-side) runner because I wanted a scarf with a ratio greater than the 8:1 factory setting.

For the first few tests I was getting a snipe at the

Figure 8-14

end of the run (**Figure 8-12**). I corrected this by adding a piece of scrap on that end for a few practice scarfs. In short order I was able to get consistent 18:1 scarfs like **Figure 8-13** without using the scrap at the end of the planer run. The snipe seemed to be caused by how the planer was held and how pressure was applied rather than something out of adjustment.

I did add one last step before glue-up, however. In **Figure 8-14** a guide for a block plane was added

Figure 8-12

Figure 8-15

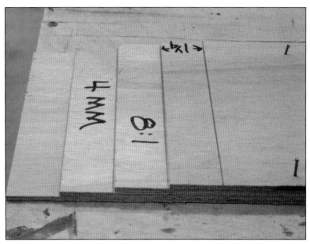

Figure 8-16

2¾ inches back from the edge of the scarf. This gave a nice clean line and recess for the edge of the opposite scarf. The drill and driver point to the line (**Figure 8-15**). It also served as a reference line to keep the two pieces square and straight.

The addition of the last step is purely a personal preference and is not necessary for the planer to cut good scarfs. In fact, any of the three over-the-counter scarfing units do a good job. Are they worth the money to buy them? Absolutely, but for the one time builder the expense may not be justified.

So if all of the over-the-counter scarfing jigs seem like too much money and the shop-made jigs too much trouble, then turn to your toolbox and pick up your ready-to-go scarfing unit—the plane. That's right, either a block plane, which I like best, or a 9- to 10-inch bench plane. I use a Bailey #3 and a Record #4 that both belonged to my father, and either a Stanley low-angle or Buck block plane.

Before you start to think how impossible it would be to cut a sloping scarf by hand, let me say that a good many boatbuilders cut scarfs just that way and by choice. I had a conversation with a British boatbuilder a number of years back; he felt

it was so easy and fast, there was no reason for him to go to the trouble of building a scarfing jig. He explained that he could cut the scarfs in the time it took to set up the jigs.

I'm not sure that I really believed him until I cut a few with a block plane. And sure enough, it was fast and easy. However, your plane must be sharp—very sharp—or it will not go smoothly or quickly. A few strokes on a stone between scarfs will do wonders for the quality of the scarfs.

Most builders seem to prefer stacking the plywood and cutting several scarfs at a time. One, it's faster, and two, the stack forms a ramp that helps cut the angle. In **Figure 8-16** the 4mm plywood has been staggered back 1¼ inches from the edge of the sheet below, and the scarf is then cut. A pencil line at 1¼ inches will help keep the slope matching its mates. Notice that the bottom sheet is flush with the table underneath. This is important—otherwise the plane can't stay at the correct angle. It takes a little practice, but acceptable scarfs can be achieved after just a few practice runs (**Figure 8-17**).

The stacking technique seems to work best if the ratio is 8:1. I haven't had a great deal of success cutting a 12:1 scarf by stacking, and I cut these one at a time. Place a piece of plywood, in this case 4mm, flush with edge of the table and strike a line 2 inches back from the edge for 12:1 scarf (**Figure 8-**

Figure 8-17

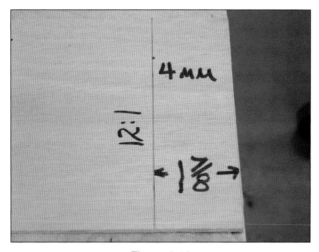

Figure 8-18

Figure 8-19

18). Then plane the forward edge down and work the slope back to the pencil line (**Figure 8-19**). At this point, I screw a guide down 1/8 inch behind the pencil line and place the plane against the guide to clean up the slope (**Figure 8-20**). The finished scarf should look like **Figure 8-21**.

I'm always pleasantly surprised by how easy it is to cut scarfs this way, but allow yourself some time to practice on scrap plywood. Don't expect to get a perfect scarf with the first try; it always takes awhile to learn a new skill. Be patient and after a bit you will be able to use the plane to cut scarfs. As you work, just think about the money you will save by learning this skill.

However, the rewards go way beyond the money you saved by cutting the scarfs by hand. There is a satisfaction that comes from mastering a task that has no monetary value. This is one of the great joys of building a boat.

There is one other way to join plywood together to make a long plank out of two shorter pieces, and it doesn't require any monetary outlay either. I first read about this method in an article written by Dynamite Payson for the now out-of-print *Small Boat Journal.* Payson just butted the ends of two pieces of plywood together and put fiberglass cloth or tape across both sides for support. Unlike Payson, who suggests using polyester resin, I recommend that you saturate the fiberglass cloth in epoxy. Also, you'll want to use a small amount of peanut-butter-thick epoxy between the edges.

Figure 8-22 shows a butt splice with peanut butter epoxy between the two edges and a layer of fiberglass cloth before being saturated with epoxy. If you choose this method, use as light a cloth as you can, like 4-ounce or 6-ounce cloth, and sand the edges of the cloth smooth once the epoxy has cured. Be sure to put freezer paper under the butt joint so the epoxy and the plywood don't become a permanent part of the table.

You will have to put the cloth on one side and

Figure 8-20

Figure 8-21

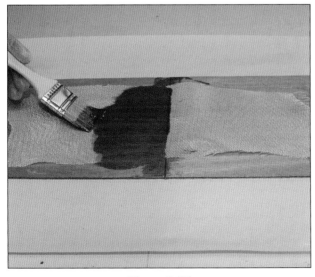

Figure 8-22

then, when the epoxy cures, apply the cloth to the opposite side. Be careful as you turn the splice over because the unsupported side will allow the splice to break.

There are those who swear by this method, but I'm not one of them. Given how easy it is to cut a scarf by hand and the excellent jigs available over the counter it's hard to justify using this method; I would counsel against it. I put it in as a fallback plan, a disaster plan in case all else fails, nothing more.

Once you settle on the scarfing method you will use—hopefully a method other than the disaster plan—the next step will be to cut the 4 x 8 sheets of plywood into smaller pieces or blanks. Ripping the sheets into smaller pieces or blanks allows the long pieces to be easily handled as they are taken on and off the boat for fitting. It also helps cut down on waste.

Each boat has a different set of blanks, and **Figure 8-23** shows how to rip the sheets of 4mm used for the planks and the 6mm for the bottom for Little Princess. The blank layouts for the 14-foot and 16-foot canoes are in the appendix with the plans.

When the 4mm blanks and the 6mm bottom are ripped and scarfed, it will be time to glue up the short pieces to make the full-length blanks. In **Figure 8-24** the individual pieces have been placed on freezer paper to keep the plywood from becoming permanently bonded to the table or surface underneath. Also, clear packing tape has been applied to each piece where the scarf starts, and in **Figure 8-25** clear tape has been applied to the opposite sides. This is an important step because the tape helps protect the plywood from the epoxy squeeze-out. The epoxy is much harder than the plywood when it cures, and having it peel off with the tape is much better than trying to sand it off.

The next step is to mix up a small batch of epoxy—about 2 ounces of resin should do it—stir the recommended 90 seconds, and brush on the

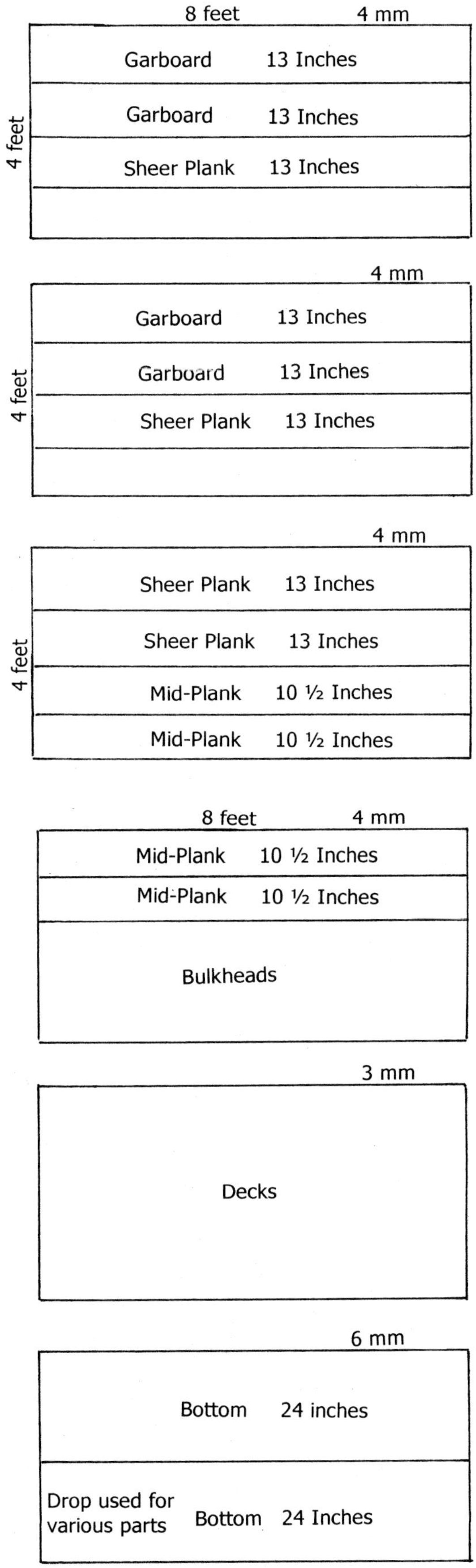
8 feet
4 mm
Garboard 13 Inches
Garboard 13 Inches
Sheer Plank 13 Inches
4 feet
4 mm
Garboard 13 Inches
Garboard 13 Inches
Sheer Plank 13 Inches
4 feet
4 mm
Sheer Plank 13 Inches
Sheer Plank 13 Inches
Mid-Plank 10 ½ Inches
Mid-Plank 10 ½ Inches
4 feet
8 feet
4 mm
Mid-Plank 10 ½ Inches
Mid-Plank 10 ½ Inches
Bulkheads
3 mm
Decks
6 mm
Bottom 24 inches
Drop used for various parts
Bottom 24 Inches

Figure 8-23

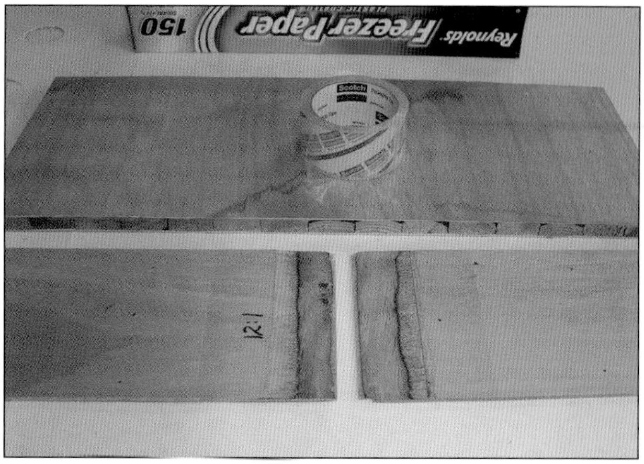

Figure 8-24

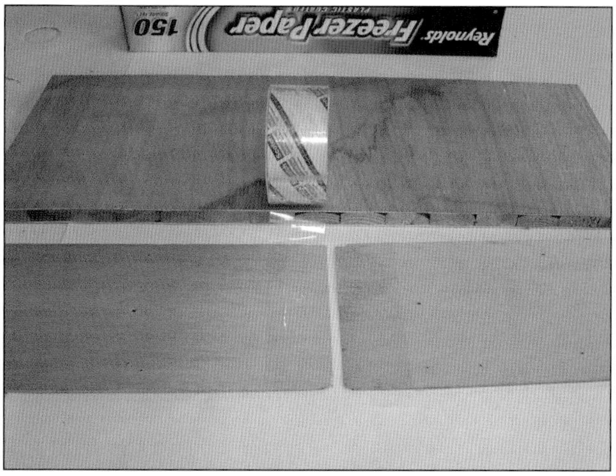

Figure 8-25

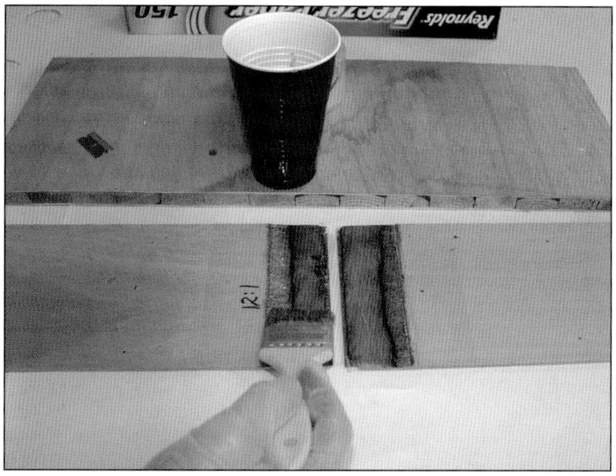

Figure 8-26

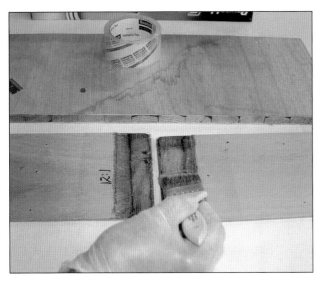

Figure 8-27

Figure 8-28

Figure 8-29

epoxy with a disposable brush (**Figure 8-26**). Next, add a small amount of silica and wood flour until a heavy cream/running catsup consistency is reached, and brush a light coat on each side (**Figure 8-27**).

I like to use a heavy cream epoxy rather than a thicker mixture when scarfing because I find the thicker epoxy creates hard spots in the plank. The heavy cream mixture comes closer to matching the stiffness of the glue between the plies.

Also, it wouldn't hurt to take some of the practice scarfs you cut and glue them up before you start on the blanks. This will give you a good idea of how much epoxy to put on and be a good test of your clamping technique.

Once both sides have a light coat of heavy cream epoxy, just flip one piece over on top of the other. I like to move the top piece around a bit to spread the epoxy. Then use the line created by the plane (see **Figure 8-7**) as a reference to square both pieces.

Be sure to wipe up the excess squeeze-out with a paper towel (**Figure 8-28**), check to be sure the pieces are square to each other, and then screw down a 1 x 8 or scrap plywood as a clamp (**Figure 8-29**). However, don't forget to put a nonstick barrier between the plywood clamp and the scarf.

I think you'll find that 6 x 1 5/8-inch coarse thread drywall screws can apply an amazing amount of clamping pressure. On wide pieces, like the bottom, I'll put several drywall screws spread across the center to distribute the clamping pressure. It's better to have a few holes in the center of the plank and get good even clamping pressure across the entire plank, because any holes created by these drywalls can be filled later with thickened epoxy.

You'll want to allow a minimum of 24 hours—in colder weather allow more time—before you remove the clamp and work on the plank. The first job will be to remove the clear tape and as much squeeze-out as possible.

Figure 8-30 shows just how much squeeze-out can be pulled up with the tape.

Once you've removed the majority of squeeze-out, take a random orbital sander with 100-grit paper and finish cleaning up the scarf (**Figure 8-31**). Exercise a bit of care with this task, because the sander can cut through the top ply fairly quickly. Should this happen, don't worry; it won't be a problem unless you plan to varnish the entire boat—and I recommend you not do that anyway.

Just be sure to support the scarf on each side by spreading your hands out a good 12 inches on either side of the scarf when picking up the blank. Turning the blank on edge will help lessen the stress on the scarf. Use another person, if possible to help handle what now resembles big limber noodles.

Also, this will be a good time to coat the entire blank with unthickened epoxy and sand it smooth. It may seem unnecessary at this point, but this will save time later. It is much easier to coat and sand the blanks while they are flat on a table or floor than on the boat.

Actually, I've found that the hour or so spent coating and sanding a blank smooth now will save about two hours of labor when putting the final finish on. Then you'll really be glad you did because you'll be in a hurry to launch the boat.

So take the time and coat each blank with a layer of epoxy, let it cure, sand it smooth, apply another coat, and sand smooth. As each blank is finished and sanded, store it in a safe out-of-the-way place until you're ready for it.

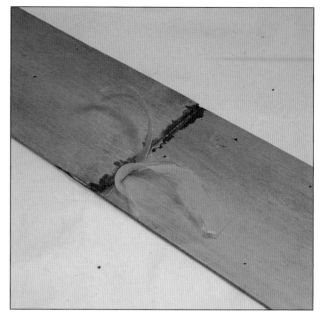

Figure 8-30

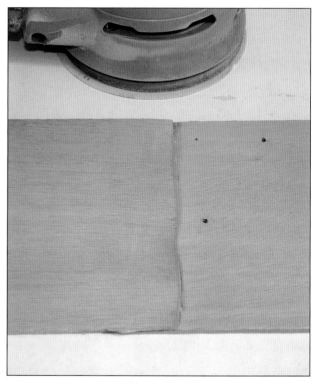

Figure 8-31

9

Setting Up the Strongback

When I set out to build my first boat, and it came time to set up the strongback, I was confused. The plans didn't really tell me what kind of strongback to build; it was assumed I had that knowledge. If I'm not mistaken, I used 2 x 8s tied together with cross-pieces and the whole unit shimmed and screwed to 2 x 4s anchored to the floor.

This would have worked well for a larger boat, but I was building a small boat and it was too close to the floor, among other issues. It was also hard to get straight and level because the 2 x 8s had some twist that I never could completely eliminate. It did the job, but there were other types of strongbacks that would have been better suited for that particular boat.

The kind of strongback I use now is a better match for small boats. Is it the only type of strongback you should use? No, there are several that would be just as good, but this particular type works well for me and will do the same for you. It's fast to build, strong, easy to keep straight, and simple to shim level.

This is a good place to mention putting 1/8-inch cheap plywood on the floor under the strongback. Building a boat is a messy process, and epoxy is very difficult to get off concrete once it hardens; the plywood is there to keep epoxy and paint off

the floor. Putting down the plywood will save many unhappy comments from the person sharing the garage or shop with you, so do this first and then assemble the strongback.

This strongback is made from a single sheet of ¾-inch 4 x 8 BC fir plywood and a single sheet of 3/8-inch BC fir plywood. Actually, if you can find both the ¾ inch and the 3/8 inch in lauan or meranti interior plywood, that will work as well and may be a little cheaper. However, the BC fir plywood can be found at any of the big chain building supply stores, while the meranti and lauan are more difficult to find. I wouldn't use MDF because it's too heavy.

While you're at the building supply store, have them rip the ¾ inch sheet into 6-inch-wide by 96-inch-long strips on their panel saw. Then have them rip the 3/8 inch sheet into 16-inch wide by 96-inch long pieces (ask them to be as accurate as possible with the 6-inch and 16-inch widths). What you should wind up with are seven 6 x 96 pieces and two 16 x 96 pieces. The drop will be a piece slightly less than 6 inches wide and a piece slightly less than 16 inches wide. The store will probably charge you a cutting fee—but it's worth it, because the panel saw will rip nice straight, square pieces.

Once these nice straight and square pieces are sitting on your shop or garage floor, you might want to ask yourself this question: "Do I plan to build more than one boat from this book?" Remember, you can build three boats from this book, and if you think you might build another boat or two, then build a 16-foot-long strongback. You may find that building a boat is sort of like eating potato chips. It's hard to eat just one potato chip, and it's hard to build just one boat.

It is easy to build boats shorter than the strongback but somewhat harder to adapt a short strongback to a longer boat. It's not impossible, just more difficult. And because this strongback will disassemble and store flat, I suggest you build the strongback 16 feet long, just in case.

The steps to assemble your strongback are the same regardless of the length, so find the drop that is less than 6 inches wide and lay it on the floor. You'll use this piece as a straight edge. Now take two 6-inch pieces, butt them end-to-end and push the straight edge against the two 6-inch-wide pieces. After you've checked to see that both sections are flush against the straight edge, place a third 6-inch section on the first two. Split the length of the top section so half is on each side of the butt joint and make sure the edges of the top section are even with the edges of the bottom two sections. Once everything is flush and even, screw the sections together using drywall screws (**Figure 9-1**). This gives you one long side for the strongback.

And after you've assembled the other side exactly the same way, lay the two pieces next to each other, cut two short sections 6 by 14½ inches from the seventh piece, and screw it together with the long sections to make a box (**Figure 9-2**). This will make a box exactly 16 inches wide by 16 feet long—or 14 feet or 12 feet, depending on the length of the side sections.

Figure 9-2

Figure 9-1

All that's left now is to screw the 3/8 inch material to the top of the box and set your strongback on sawhorses or shop-made boxes, like in **Figure 9-3**. The top surface of the strongback should 30 to 36 inches above the floor. The shop-made boxes are 24 inches high; that seems to work best for me.

Figure 9-3

It probably wouldn't be a bad idea, at this point, to check the strongback for level in both directions. If you find a low spot, use shims to bring it to level. Generally a high spot will mean shimming on either side of high to get level. Once everything is level for both the length and width, use drywall screws to lock it down on the boxes or sawhorses.

Now with the strongback level and screwed down, mark the centerline (8 inches if the strongback is 16 inches wide) at both ends, as in **Figure 9-4**.

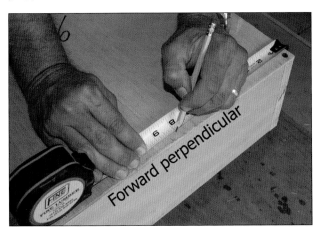

Figure 9-4

Then start placing a mark at each station. For example, Station #1 is 1-4-0 or 1 foot 4 0/8 inches back from the front edge of the strongback (**Figure 9-5**).

Figure 9-5

Remember, the forward edge of the strongback is also the forward perpendicular or the very front of the boat, and **all measurements are taken from the forward perpendicular**. Each station will be a specific distance back from the forward perpendicular. So Station #1 is 1-4-0 feet, Station #2 is 3-4-0 and so forth back toward the stern or back of the boat (**Figure 9-6**). Notice that the marks for the stations are made on or very close to the centerline of the strongback. This is more accurate than measuring down one side or the other, because if the strongback is slightly out of square, the distance would be thrown off.

The distance of all the stations or the station spacing for each boat can be found on the plans in the appendix. These distances should be carefully transferred to the strongback, and the station number clearly noted by each mark.

Perhaps I should qualify what I mean by *care-*

Figure 9-6

Figure 9-7

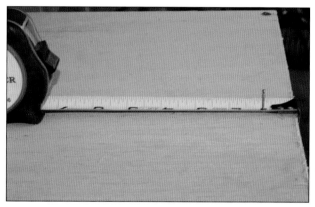

Figure 9-8

fully transferred. Make your measurements as accurately as possible but worry less about 1/32 inch and more about double-checking that 1-4-0 is 1 foot 4 inches and not 1 foot 3 inches or 1 foot 4½ inches. It is kind of hard to make a mistake at Station #1 (I've done it, however) and much easier to put Station #2 at 2-4-0 instead of 3-4-0 (I've done that too).

So worry about the big errors and not about an error of 1/32 inch. It is the unusual boatbuilder who works to 1/32. I personally know a builder who works to a 1/64 inch, and to my knowledge he has not finished either boat he has started. Remember, the measurements are given to the 1/8 inch, not to 1/32 or 1/64 inch. Don't be completely and totally exacting; just be careful as you measure each station from the forward perpendicular.

And after each station has been carefully marked, take a square and draw a line about 4

inches long on the centerline at both ends of the strongback (**Figure 9-7**). Then set your tape on the forward edge of the strongback and drive a finish nail in the small hole in the tape, as in **Figure 9-8**. This small nail will keep the measuring tape in place while you make sure each 1½ x 16 x ¾ cleat (**Figure 9-9**) is square to the centerline. The station molds will be screwed to these cleats so it's important they are square to the centerline of the strongback, which is, of course, the centerline of the boat.

It's not only important that the cleats are square but also important which side of the station mark/line they go. In **Figure 9-10** the cleat for Station #1 is placed forward, toward the bow, of the mark. Station #2, Station #3, and Station #4 are all forward of the station mark/line as well. Notice that a

Figure 9-9

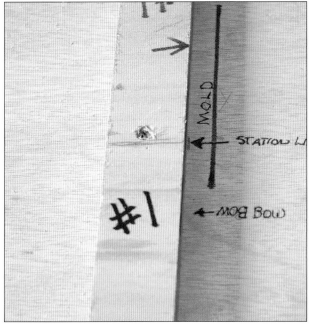

Figure 9-10

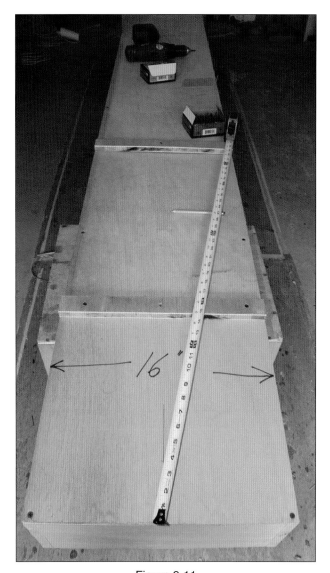

Figure 9-11

end on the diagonal, and make any small adjustments until both dimensions are the same, in this case 39 5/16 (**Figures 9-12** and **9-13**). Once you are satisfied that the two measurements are the same, set two more drywall screws to lock it all down (**Figure 9-14**). Also, I find this is a good time to double-check the measurement of the station spacing from the forward perpendicular. I've caught a mistake or two at this point, and I've never been sorry I took the time to double-check.

Placing the cleat on the forward side of the station line puts the forward edge of the station mold resting on the station line. This puts the back edge of the station mold inside the curve of the plank

drywall screw is set at the center of the cleat. This is done so it will be easier to adjust the cleat for square.

To check for square: Measure one end of the cleat on the diagonal (**Figure 9-11**), then the other

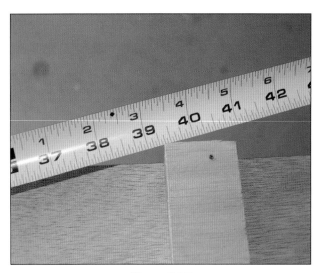

Figure 9-12

Figure 9-13

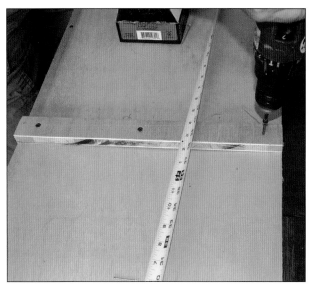

Figure 9-14

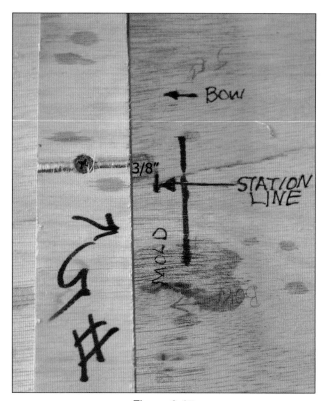

Figure 9-15

where it doesn't interfere and keep the plank from lying fair.

Station molds #1 through #4 have their forward edges on the station line, but the mold for Station #5 splits the station line. This means the cleat needs to be one half the thickness of the mold in front of the station line. In this case it's 3/8 inch because the mold material is ¾ inch thick (**Figure 9-15**). When mold #5 is screwed to the cleat, the station line will fall in the middle of the mold.

The cleat for Station #6, unlike #5, falls aft of the station line or toward the back of the strong-back (**Figure 9-16**). All of this can get a little confusing, so I always put an arrow on the side of the cleat that gets the mold. As many boats as I've built, I still have to stop and think about which side the mold goes on; putting the arrows down now keeps

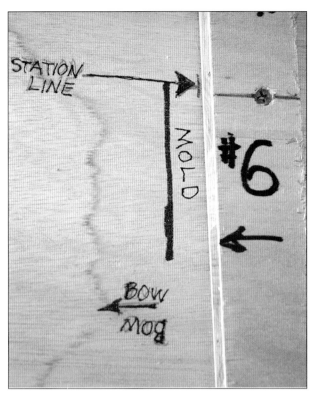

Figure 9-16

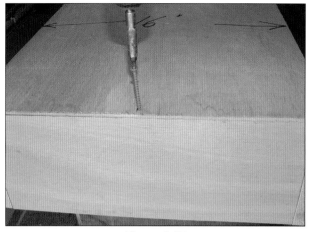

Figure 9-17

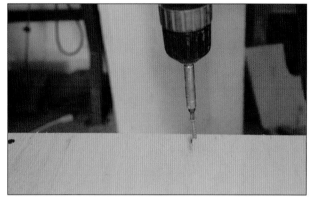

Figure 9-18

me from attaching the mold to the wrong side. The cleats for Stations #6, #7, and #8 all fall on the aft or back side of the station line and are squared the same way as #5 through #1.

At this point it's time to put a centerline on each of the cleats. When I did this the first time, I just measured over one half the width of the cleat and put a mark, but this didn't work because the strongback had a slight curve. All I did was reproduce the slight curve. What I should have done was go to each end of the strongback and put a drywall screw just to one side of the centerline. Make sure both drywall screws are on the same side and just touch the line (**Figures 9-17** and **9-18**). Then string a chalk line between the drywall screws like **Figure 9-19**. Be sure that you wrap the string so it is directly over the centerline (**Figure 9-20**).

Figure 9-19

Figure 9-20

Figure 9-21

Figure 9-22

Now transfer the line to the cleats. I prefer to do this with a pencil mark directly under the string, like **Figure 9-21**. I tried snapping the chalk line but found that was too fuzzy. I like to use a square so the centerline is the full width of the cleat (**Figure 9-22**).

Once the last centerline is on the cleats, sit back and admire your accomplishment. Remember, boatbuilding is a series of achievements to be enjoyed. Setting up the strongback was a major step forward toward completing the boat.

10

Putting the Molds on the Strongback

Now that all the cleats are on the strongback and everything is marked with centerlines and station numbers, you are ready to put the molds on the strongback. **Figure 10-1** shows the strongback ready for station mold #1.

Figure 10-1

Remember from chapter 9 that the cleats on #1, #2, #3, and #4 all went forward of the station mark; that was so the forward edge of the mold would fall on the station line. **Figure 10-2** is a close-up of Station #1 and shows the cleat forward (toward the bow) of the station line; the black line shows where the mold will sit. I suggest you mark each station like this—it helps reduce mistakes, particularly when you're working intermittently. I've put the mold on the wrong side of the cleat more than once when distracted.

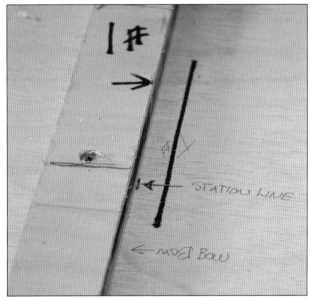

Figure 10-2

In **Figure 10-3** station mold #1 is in place, and two drywall screws hold it to the cleat. The centerline on the face was lined up with the centerline on the cleat before it was screwed in place.

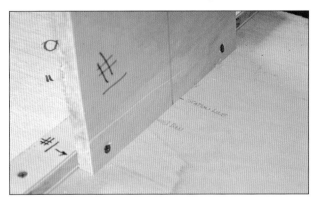

Figure 10-3

Figure 10-4

Figure 10-5

Treat #3 and #4 the same as #1 and #2 by putting the station mold aft of the cleat. Use a clamp
to hold it as you align the centerlines and screw it
down. This should go fairly quickly, particularly by
using a clamp as an extra pair of hands.

Stations #1 through #4 all have the cleat forward
of the station mark, and so does Station #5, but #5
is 3/8 inch (one half the width of the mold material)
in front of the cleat, as shown in **Figure 10-6**. The
black line indicates the position of the mold. This
was done so the station line would fall in the center of the mold rather than the forward edge of #1
through #4.

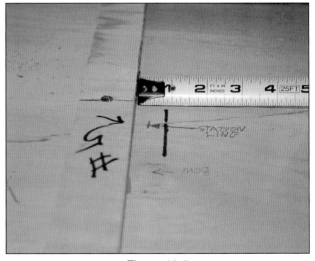
Figure 10-6

Station mold #2 has its bulkhead nailed to it and
is attached to the cleat so the bulkhead faces the bow
(**Figure 10-4**). Notice that the nails are positioned
toward the sheer. This makes it easy to reach up
under the boat and pull the nails when the boat is
ready to turn over. Nothing is more frustrating than
having the boat stuck on the molds because of a
hard-to-reach nail. **Remember: Every nail in the
boat is temporary and will be pulled. So always
leave enough to pull, in a place that is easy to reach.**

You'll want to place the centerline of station
mold #2 on the centerline of the cleat before you
screw it in place with drywall screws (**Figure 10-5**).
I like to use a clamp or a spring clamp to hold the
mold in place while I tap it into alignment. Even
then the drywall can pull it off a little, so check
before you move on to #3 and #4.

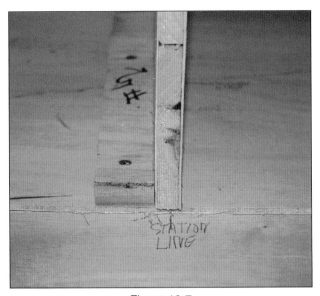

Figure 10-7

Figure 10-9

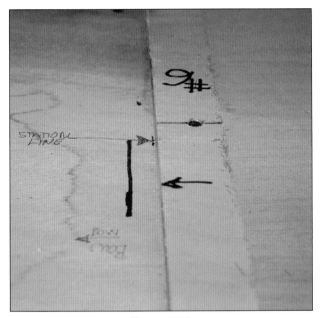

Figure 10-8

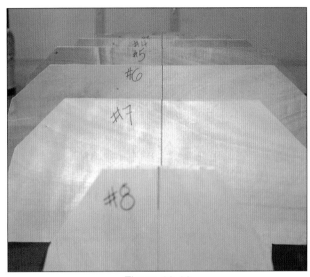

Figure 10-10

Figure 10-7 shows the relationship of the station line to the mold.

After #5 there is a change again: At #6 the mold goes forward, toward the bow, and the cleat is aft of the station line. **Figure 10-8** is a close-up of Station #6, with the black line indicating where the mold sits. **Figure 10-9** shows the mold screwed to the cleat and where the station line is in relationship to the mold and cleat. Stations #6, #7, and #8 are all set up the same way as shown in **Figure 10-9**.

Remember, Station #7 has a bulkhead, and that

bulkhead is on the side of the mold that faces toward the stern of the boat. The bulkhead should be nailed to the mold, and just like #2 the nails are kept toward the sheer so they can be easily reached.

Once #7 and #8 are screwed in place, you will need to check that the centerlines of the molds are aligned. In **Figure 10-10** mold #8 is slightly to the left; the rest are lined up. I unscrewed #8 and used a clamp to hold it while I taped the mold in line with the rest (**Figure 10-11**). The bulkhead at #7 has been removed for better visibility.

I've found that one or two molds being slightly out is not uncommon, but if you have one or two

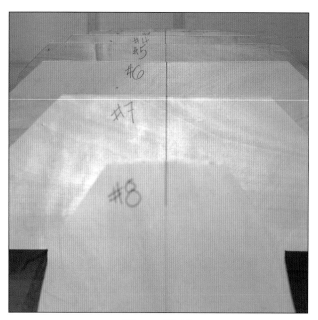

Figure 10-11

that are way off you will want to check and see why. Generally a centerline that is way off has been marked incorrectly on the mold or on the cleat. But it will be important to find the reason and correct it before continuing.

I suppose the main thing to remember is not to be a slave to the line on the strongback. It's far more important that the centerlines on the molds are in alignment, as in **Figure 10-11**.

The last step, after everything is aligned, will be to tape all the edges of the molds so they don't get epoxied to the boat (**Figure 10-12**). I like to use 2-inch blue masking tape because I can tell at a glance if everything is taped. However, you don't want to tape the edges of the bulkheads—those are supposed to be part of the boat. Just pull the bulkheads out a bit on the nails and slip the tape in between the bulkhead and the mold. When you're finished, push the bulkhead back against the mold. You're ready to move on to setting the stems.

Figure 10-12

11

Putting the Stems on the Strongback

Setting the stems is the last task to be done before you start to plank in the boat. I don't remember when I started setting the stems using this method, but I've been doing it this way for a long time. More than likely I saw it done this way somewhere and just incorporated it into the way I build boats.

There's nothing complicated about the way I secure the stems. It works very well on boats with a flat bottom, both large and small.

The method uses a rectangle that represents height above the strongback and the distance back from the forward perpendicular for the heel of the stem. **Figure 11-1** shows a rectangle and the bow stem with the sheer, upper chine, lower chine, and heel (A) all clearly marked. The rectangle is 1-9-2 tall by 0-7-6 wide. The distance 1-9-2 is derived by subtracting the distance the heel of the bow stem is above the baseline (0-2-6) from the height of the baseline above the strongback (24 inches or 1-11-8). The measurement 0-7-6 is the distance the heel of the stem is back from the forward perpendicular. This information is on the plans at the back of the book.

So if you think of the side of the rectangle with 1-9-2 written on it as the forward perpendicular (the forward edge of the strongback) and the side labeled strongback as the strongback, then the top corner that is 0-7-6 back is where the heel of the stem should be.

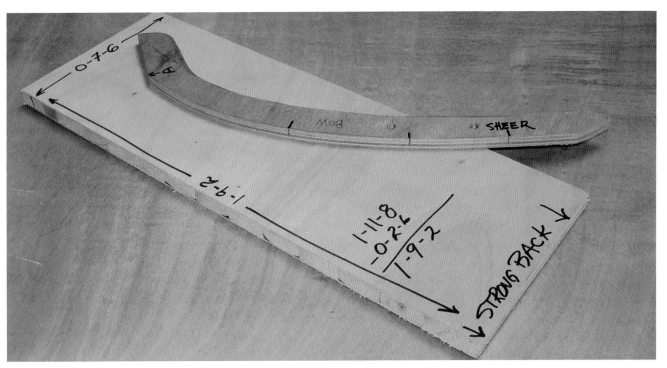

Figure 11-1

In **Figure 11-2** point A has been located on that corner and the stem pivoted forward until the sheer intersects the forward edge. Once in position, you'll want to secure it with a drywall screw and draw lines clearly marking the location.

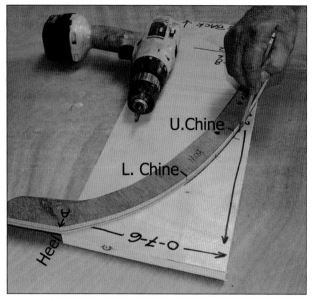

Figure 11-2

Obviously if you were to put this on the strongback now, the rectangle would interfere with the planking of the boat. So you'll want to trim off the area above the lower chine tick mark just like in **Figure 11-3**. Use the pencil marks to relocate the stem in exactly the same place and secure it with a couple of drywall screws. Now when the stem is located on the strongback, the garboards can be put on and the rectangle won't interfere—yet the heel of the stem is held captive at the correct point.

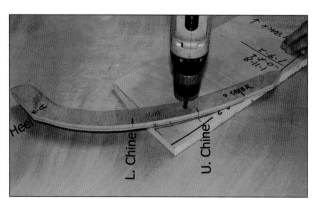

Figure 11-3

The heel of the stem needs to be on the centerline of the boat as well. That means a cleat will need to be located the thickness of the rectangle and half the thickness of the stem over from the centerline of the boat. In **Figure 11-4** that distance shows to be 7/8 inch.

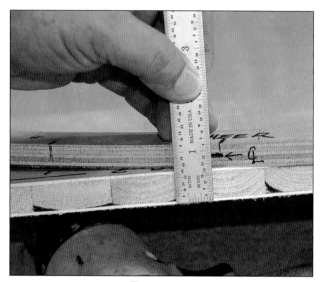

Figure 11-4

Figure 11-5

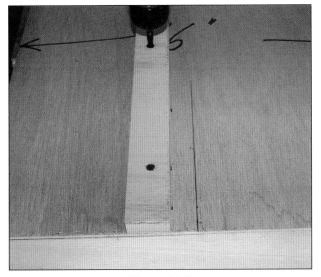

Figure 11-6

Figure 11-7

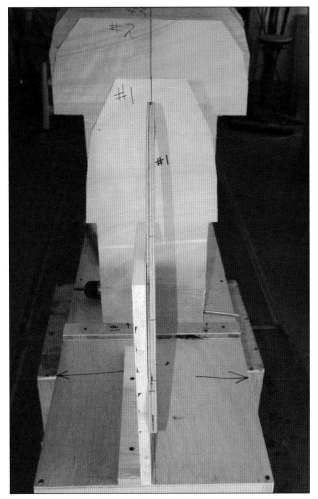

Figure 11-8

In **Figure 11-5** tick marks are placed 7/8 inch over from the centerline, a cleat is set on those marks (**Figure 11-6**), and the stem assembly is screwed to that cleat (**Figure 11-7**). This places the center of the stem on the centerline of the boat.

You'll want to be sure that heel of the stem lines up with the centerline of the molds as in **Figure 11-8**.

Figure 11-9

Figure 11-9 shows the forward edge of the rectangle even with the front of the strongback and secured to the side cleat. Once the bottom and the garboards are permanently on the boat, the assembly can be removed so the middle plank can be placed.

All that is left to do, at this point, is repeat the process for the stern stem—only the rectangle for the stern assembly is 1-9-4 high and 0-7-4 wide. You'll find the needed information on the plans in the appendix.

Now you're ready to start assembling the boat. All the blanks are scarfed and ready, so progress will seem faster and more visibly concrete. The multitude of parts you have been making are sitting on the strongback, coalesced into the skeleton of the boat.

It's far easier to imagine what the finished boat will look like and easier to see yourself paddling some distant lake, watching the breeze ripple the water. Easier to feel the boat slide across the ripples.

12

Putting on the Bottom and Cutting the Bevel

The first task you'll want to do is strike a center-line on the scarfed bottom. The bottom is 24 inches wide, so measure over 12 inches from one side and place a series of tick marks down the length of the bottom. Then, using those marks, take a long straight edge and strike a centerline (**Figure 12-1**).

Figure 12-1

It will be more important for the line to be straight than to be in the exact center of the bottom. If your plank is 24 1/8 or 24 1/16 just measure over the 12 inches from the same side and don't worry about the 1/8 or 1/16 of an inch. Also, if the two pieces aren't exactly square to each other, you'll need to measure over 12 inches at each end and then, just like you did on the strongback, use a snap line to strike the centerline. This will create a straight line in spite of the planks not being square.

Once you're satisfied that the line is straight and clear, place the bottom on top of the molds with the line down. Make any adjustments so the centerline on the bottom is over the centerline of the molds. When you have everything fairly close, then center the bottom over Station #1 like **Figure 12-2**.

Figure 12-2

Then, using a square to true up the station mold, set a small finish nail to hold the bottom in place (**Figure 12-3**). Now move to Station #8 and do the same thing.

With the two ends held in place with finish nails, check the alignment at each station. You will probably find small discrepancies like **Figure 12-4**. Sometimes you can just bump the side of the strongback one way or the other to correct things. If not, unscrew the mold and tap it over until it

61

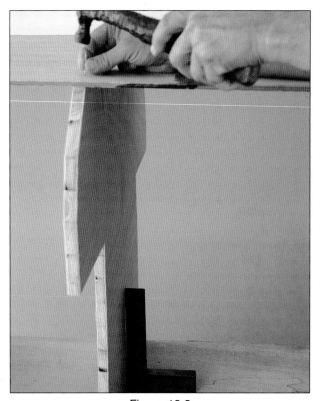

Figure 12-3

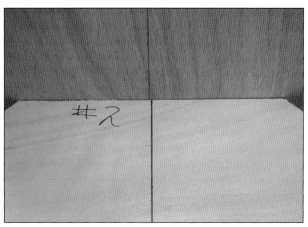

Figure 12-4

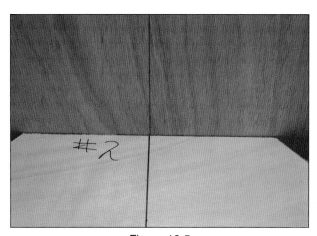

Figure 12-5

lines up (**Figure 12-5**). There shouldn't be any big variation but if there is, stop and figure out what caused it. I find the most common cause is a curve in the strongback; just bumping it over will help get things back in alignment.

When the molds have been tapped and bumped so the lines on the bottom and mold match, set a finish nail to lock each mold and bottom together. Be sure to use a square like you did for #1 and #8 —it's important that everything be square. Also, you'll want to attach the stem to the bottom with a countersunk #6 x ¾ stainless-steel or bronze screw. This will pull the bottom down to the stem and help hold the stem in alignment.

Now with everything nailed down, start at the point where the heel of the stem strikes the bottom and put a mark on either side of the stem. Be sure to get a clear mark where the heel strikes the bottom. Then move on to Station #1 and put a mark on either side of the bottom along with the station number. You'll want to do this for each station (**Figure 12-6**). Be sure to put the station number by the tick marks: That makes it easier to reposition the bottom in the right place.

Figure 12-6

The next step is to pull the bottom off and connect all those tick marks with a batten. In **Figure 12-7** the bottom is on a flat surface and the 9/16 x 11/16 fir batten has been sprung so it touches all the marks. I like to start with the batten on Station #5 —more or less in the middle—and work my way toward each end.

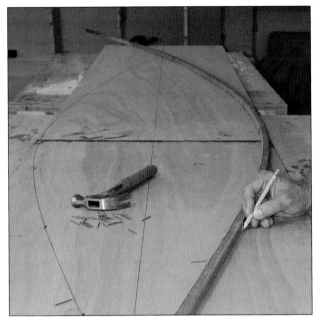

Figure 12-7

Just be sure to check that the batten is touching each mark and then draw the line. **Figure 12-8** shows how the line should fall on the mark.

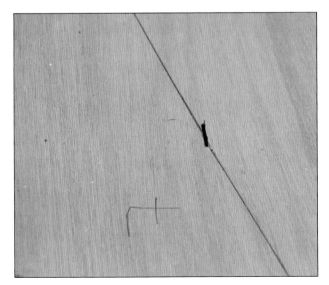

Figure 12-8

What happens if the batten doesn't line up with the marks? In **Figure 12-9** notice that there are two lines on the left side. The first line was where the batten was touching the mark, but that line missed the point where the stem heel sat on the bottom. When I noticed that, I moved the batten, even though it fell outside the station mark. The point is not to be a slave to the station marks, and if you see an obvious mistake, let the batten fall outside the mark.

Figure 12-9

All you're doing here is cutting the rough shape of the bottom and cutting away most of the excess plywood. Rather than cut right on the line you'll want to cut about ¼ to ½ inch outside the line (**Figure 12-9**). This will give a little wiggle room, which I find is always welcome when the bottom goes back on the molds and is accurately centered up again. However, more than ½ inch outside the line won't be necessary and makes for more work as the bevel is cut.

At first glance you'd think that the line you just marked would be the final shape of the bottom, but this isn't the case.

The drawing in **Figure 12-10** shows why. The section labeled A needs to be cut off so the garboard (the plank adjacent to the bottom) can lie flat against the station mold. Extending the line of the station mold up through the bottom will give you a cross section of the area to be removed. And if you do that at each station, you'll have a series of points that give you the inside shape of the bottom.

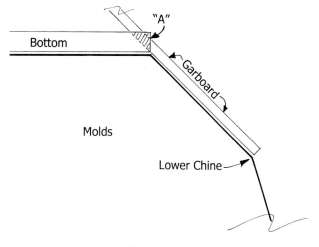

Figure 12-10

Using a Japanese saw to carry that line up through the bottom is a fast and easy method (**Figure 12-11**). Just remember to keep the saw parallel to the chine. If you rock the saw forward the cut will be too deep and will not be an accurate point.

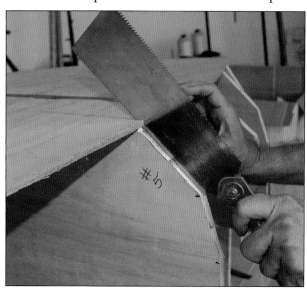

Figure 12-11

I like to start at Station #5 and work my way toward either end of the boat. Also, putting a pencil mark at the end of the cut will make it much easier to see when springing a batten.

And springing a batten is the next step (**Figure 12-12**). I find it much easier to handle the batten if I start at Station #5, then set #4, then #6, and so on, working back and forth from the centerline. **Figure 12-13** is a close-up of the cut, tick mark, and batten, and that's how the batten should line up at each station.

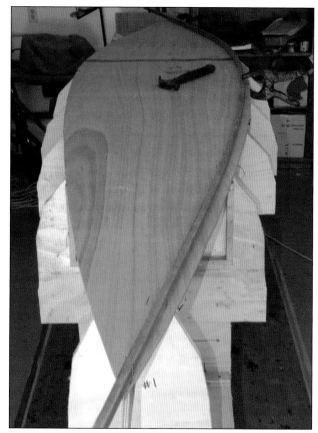

Figure 12-12

Notice, too, that the saw cut is on the station line and not the center of the mold. You'll probably find it easier to make the cut right on the edge of the mold so it can act as a guide for the proper angle of the saw. What happens if you make the cut in the center of the mold or close to the center? Nothing, really—the difference between the two points is very small, but it will be better and more

Figure 12-13

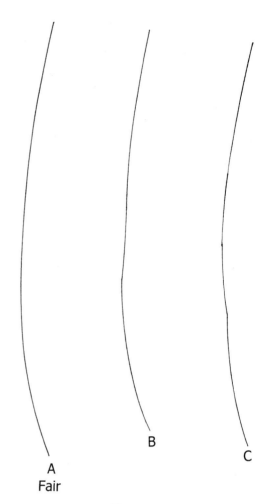

A
Fair

Figure 12-14

accurate to be close to station line. When you are satisfied that the batten is accurate and fair, draw the line, and then do the same on the other side of the boat.

You don't have to be in boatbuilding very long to run into the word *fair*. This is a very subjective word, like *pretty* or *delicious*. And pretty, as well as delicious, is in the eye or mouth of the individual doing the describing. So just what is a fair line exactly? **Figure 12-14** has three lines: One is a sweeping, continuous curve, and the other two have either a hollow or a hump. Try to imagine water flowing along all three curves; it's not difficult to see that first curve will be the best. A very well-known designer once said that "Water doesn't like to be surprised," and both B and C have surprises for water. What you should do, then, is let your eye flow along the batten line and look for surprises. If there are none, then it's a fair line.

It is important that the lines on both sides of the boat are fair and symmetrical: This is the line that you'll trim to when cutting the bevel on the bottom. Cutting the bevel can be tricky because it changes from one point to another. Builders have devised some very ingenious jigs to speed up this process and at the same time make it more accurate. I read about one jig that used a router mounted in a carrier that changed angle as the jig was pushed along the bottom or plank. There are others equally as ingenious and complicated, but they don't apply here.

Certainly the system I use is neither ingenious nor complicated. It's just a variation on a jig I read about a number of years ago. It consists of two parts: a 5/8 x ¾-inch batten and a plane with an attachment on the side.

Figure 12-15 shows the batten attached to the molds just above the lower chine. This will act as a guide for the plane, which is the other part of the system (**Figure 12-16**). You make the attachment to the dimensions shown in **Figure 12-17**. Also, **Figure 12-17** shows the relationship of the batten and attachment. Because the batten is 5/8 and the height of the attachment's bar is also 5/8, the surface of the batten and the sole of the plane are parallel.

Figure 12-18 shows the plane cutting the bevel. Notice that the bevel is cut right to the line. Having

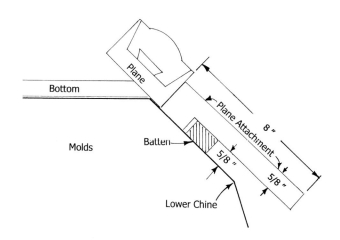

Figure 12-17

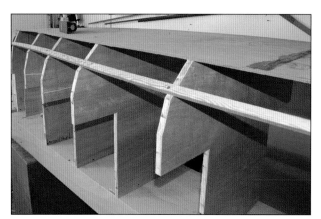

Figure 12-15

Figure 12-16

Figure 12-18

the line marked on the bottom is important so you don't plane off too much and create a hollow. Even with the line, it's easy to cut off too much, so take your time and step back frequently to make sure the line of the bottom is being planed fair.

When both sides of the bottom are beveled, take the time to look at what you've accomplished. The bottom started as a large flimsy rectangle of plywood, and you've turned it into the bottom of your boat. Not only that, you've cut a bevel that changed the entire length of the boat and created a matching surface for the garboards. Now, that's something to be proud of.

13

Hanging the Garboards

Figure 13-2

With the bottom beveled, your next step is to hang the garboards. This process isn't much different from putting the bottom on. You start with a long flimsy rectangle and when you're finished, you have the garboard planks for your boat. However, with the garboards there is no centerline—you simply temporarily attach the blank to the molds as in **Figures 13-1** and **13-2**. Notice that the blank is well centered with about 10 inches extending above #5 and 3 or 4 inches above the bow and stern.

I like to start at #5 and set a single nail in the

mold, then work toward each end. As you move from Station #4 to #6 and the other stations, make sure the plywood lies against the bottom as well as the molds. This will take a bit of juggling and shifting the blank around. In the beginning it will seem that it simply won't work, but move the blank in small increments and you'll get it to lie against the hull. I generally have to pull all the nails and start over two or three times before I get it to lie up against the molds and bottom. I've done this many times without help, but a spare pair of hands is always welcome.

When that is accomplished, place a pencil mark at the lower chine or the break in the chine. **Figure**

Figure 13-1

13-3 shows where the pencil mark is at the lower chine for Station #2. From Station #2 move to each station and put a pencil mark at the lower chine. I like to mark each side of the mold at the same time because this helps reposition the blank in the same location. Also, be sure to put the tick mark on the side of the mold that is the station line. In **Figure 13-3**, the tick mark is on the station line, but if the tick mark was on the other side of the mold, it would be off a small amount.

Figure 13-3

Figure 13-5

Once you've marked each station, then place a continuous line where the bottom meets the garboard (**Figure 13-4**). Make this solid and clearly visible because it will be an important reference

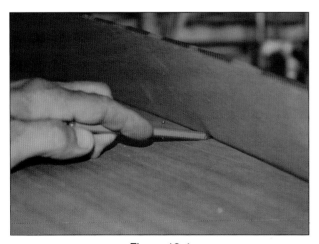

Figure 13-4

line. Another important reference point is where the bow and stern fall on the garboard, so mark that point clearly as well.

Now that the blank is clearly marked, it's time to turn the blank into a garboard plank. So pull it off the boat, lay it on a flat surface, and connect all those tick marks with a batten just like you did on the bottom.

Be sure to support the scarf as you take the blank off the boat. Also, after a few boats I learned that it was much easier to start pulling the nails at each end and work toward the center, or Station #5. This helped control that big flimsy piece of plywood, particularly if I was working alone. Another trick I discovered was to turn the edge up as I carried the blank. This removed a great deal of stress on the scarf.

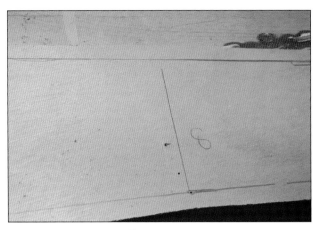
Figure 13-6

Figure 13-8

You'll want to start at #5 as you spring the batten to connect the tick marks, alternating a station on either side as you move toward the ends. **Figure 13-5** shows the batten sprung and a line drawn so the plank can be cut out of the blank.

However, you'll want to just rough-cut the plank at first. In **Figure 13-6** the cut is made about ¾ inch outside the line on both sides. Notice the line drawn along the station mold and the station number by the line. All this information will make it much simpler to put the rough-cut plank back on the molds in the same spot.

Figure 13-7 shows the rough-cut plank up on the strongback to check the fit. The plank needs to go back in the exact position where it was initially marked, and the lines at the stations and chines will make this possible (**Figure 13-8**). The line where the bottom joins the garboard has also been used in

Figure 13-9

Figure 13-9. It's important that the plank lie against the bottom (like **Figure 13-9**) for the entire length of the bottom and that it lie against each station mold (**Figure 13-8**). There have been times when I've had to adjust and readjust a rough plank for 30 minutes or so in order to get it just right. Take your time, be patient, and remember: Small movements can make big changes.

I've found that small, sometimes very small, movements toward either the bow or stern will cause everything to line up on marks and lie completely flat against the molds. I like to center everything on Station #5, set one nail, and then work toward the bow and the stern. Having a single nail at #5 allows the bow or the stern to be shifted up or down to get the plank to lie flat. There are many times I've been very glad to have that ¾ inch extra, because it gave room for some fine-tuning of the rough plank.

Figure 13-7

If you find that you need to shift the lines for the plank to lie fair (and this is not unusual), then place new tick marks, pull off the plank, and strike a new line. **It would be very wise to put the rough plank back up on the strongback for one final check before you trim down to the line.**

When you're satisfied that the plank is in the correct position, then pull the plank off and trim down to the line. Cut about 1/32 to 1/16 outside the line and plane down to the line. This will give a smooth fair line that you can't get by cutting with a saw. Don't trim the edge that extends over the bottom. That will be trimmed off after the garboard has been set with epoxy.

Now put the trimmed garboard back on the boat starting at #5 and working toward the ends. The plank should fall right on the lower chine (**Figure 13-10**) at each station and lie against the bottom.

Figure 13-11

Figure 13-12

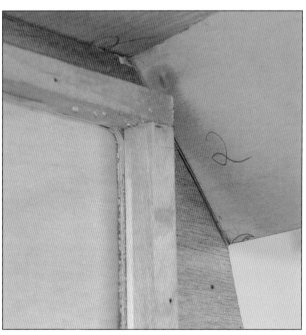

Figure 13-10

It would seem that the plank wouldn't come off the strongback anymore, but you'll want to take it off one more time. This won't be a difficult process if you will set a nail at each station so the nail just touches the bottom edge of the plank (**Figure 13-11**). The nail and the arrow at each station will allow

the plank to be quickly dropped back into position.

At this point it would be good to mention that you may have found that the plank didn't fall exactly on the lower chine after the final trim. I rarely have the plank line up with each and every lower chine. Both **Figures 13-12** and **13-13** show some variation in where the plank falls on the mold. A small amount of variation won't really have any effect on the shape of the hull.

Figure 13-13

You may also find that the plank doesn't lie tight against the mold without creating an unfair hollow in the plank. I have found that it's better to allow the plank to stand out from the mold slightly rather than put a hollow in the plank. There is an old saying in boatbuilding that "the plank must lie fair"—which is just another way of saying, Let it stand out a bit rather than create an unfair line.

I've seen it be a perfect fit on one side and stand out from a mold on the other. This is what you may find when you take the plank off and hang it on the other side. **Figure 13-14** shows the first plank hung on the opposite side. Now the lines you marked at the station molds will be on the outside. Use them to line up on Station #5 and the others. Having the lines from the other side not exactly match up to the station molds on this side is not cause for alarm (**Figure 13-15**). I've found this to be the case more often than not, but just remember that it's more important for the plank to lie fair than to match a line.

I think it's also good to remember that the boat and the strongback are not really symmetrical. There is a slight variation from side to side no matter how carefully you measure and lay things out. And that's the reason you will have slight discrepancies like **Figure 13-15**.

Figure 13-14

Figure 13-15

Figure 13-16

Figure 13-17

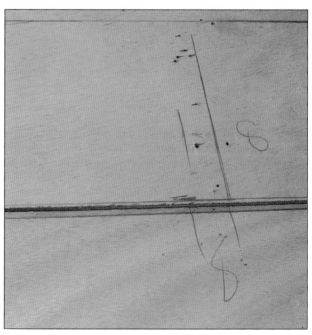

Figure 13-18

What you really want to see is if the plank will hang properly on this side. If the plank falls on all the chines like **Figure 13-16** and lies against the full length of the bottom, then the next step is easy. Just lay this plank over the blank for the other garboard, nail it down, and trace around it (**Figure 13-17**). Be sure to transfer all the station molds and numbers to the blank before you lift the first plank off (**Figure 13-18**). You'll want to copy all that information to inside the line so it won't be cut off. The next step is to cut 1/32 outside the line and then plane down to the line. I like the small, easy-to-handle block plane for this job.

But what if the first plank didn't really work on the other side? Well, if it wasn't off by much—and it shouldn't be—then cut about an inch outside the line and fit it just like you did the first plank. Actually if you have been careful about laying out the strongback and molds, this won't be a problem. It's happened to me a couple of times, but I believe that I never got a good fit on the first side, so naturally the plank wasn't going to work the other side. Either I was in a hurry or I wasn't paying attention, or both.

You, on the other hand, are paying attention, are not in a hurry, and have been very careful about the layout, so just plane down to the line and put the plank on the strongback. In **Figure 13-19** both planks are on the strongback and the excess at the bow is being trimmed off. The handy little saw being used is a Japanese keyhole saw—it's perfect for this type of job. Notice the drywall screw set toward the bottom; there is also one hidden by the saw. These hold the garboard tight against the stem and stern.

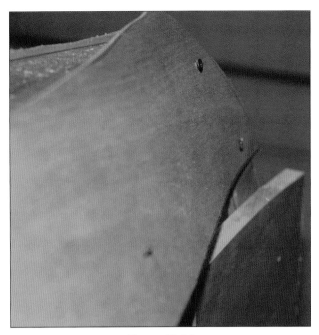
Figure 13-20

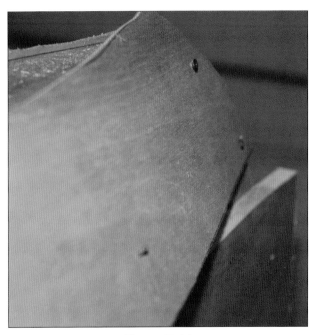
Figure 13-21

Figure 13-19

However, drywall screws have a great deal of power and can pull the plank out of fair (**Figure 13-20**). **Figure 13-21** shows the same screw after it has been backed out a bit.

Now is a good time to set a nail where the edge of the second plank falls on the mold. This will be at the chine or very close to it, just like in **Figure 13-11**. Having those reference nails in place will make gluing the plank in place much easier.

In **Figure 13-22** both planks are in place, and four drywall screws hold the planks against the stem. There are four screws at the stern as well. Notice that the bottom edges of the garboards (the top edges, really, because the boat is upside down) don't match. They both are below the chine mark on the stem, and that's what is most important. The mid-plank lap will cover both ends, so it's not something you have to worry about. The most important issue is that both planks have a fair and pleasing line.

Figure 13-22

Once both planks are lying fair, they're ready to epoxy in place. There's nothing startling about the way I epoxy a plank. It's very straightforward, really. Just start at the bow (there's no reason to start at the bow, it's just my preference) and remove all the nails back to and including Station #5. Make sure that #6, #7, and #8 all have two nails each at the station mold. This keeps the plank locked in place and keeps it from shifting. Then gently bend the plank out away from the strongback. Here's where an extra pair of hands really help—but a stick, used as a jam, will accomplish the same thing. (See **Figure 13-28**, page 76.)

Obviously, if you bend the plank too much it will snap, so use some judgment about how far to

bend it out. I bend it out just enough to work and no more. It's probably not more than 24 to 30 inches at the maximum. You might find you can work at 12 to 18 inches, which will be better.

When the jam is in place, or the extra pair of hands, mix about 3 ounces of resin and the appropriate amount of hardener. Then, using a disposable brush, coat the stem, the edge of the bottom, and the plank where it will come in contact with the stem and bottom (**Figure 13-23**). If you don't pre-coat these areas with unthickened epoxy (just like pre-coating the scarf joints), the end grain of the plywood will absorb the epoxy from the thickened mixture and glue-starve the joint. And a glue-

Figure 13-23

Figure 13-24

starved joint is a weak joint.

There should be enough epoxy left in the cup to add the silica and wood flour for a peanut butter mixture. Start with small amounts of silica until you get the right consistency. Then place a small amount of the thickened mixture along the bottom. The idea is to have just enough to bond the garboard to the bottom and the stems. Actually, you'll want to be fairly generous with the epoxy on the stems. **Figure 13-24** shows the approximate amount of thickened epoxy to place along the bottom edge. Notice that there is a gap where the mold is. I've learned that not putting the epoxy over the mold makes cleanup much easier.

Keep putting epoxy on the bottom until you reach the area between Station #5 and Station #6. Stop about halfway between the two stations, pull the jam so the plank lies against the hull, and nail it into place (**Figure 13-25**). Start at #5 and work toward the bow. Just be sure the bottom edge of the plank lines up with the reference nails (**Figure 13-26**).

Once the plank is nailed down, it will be important to take a rag and wipe up the squeeze-out on the underside of the hull (**Figure 13-27**). Failing to wipe up the excess epoxy before it cures will create a series of problems as construction on the boat progresses. The problems are nothing serious, but they will create extra work sanding and finishing out the boat. So now is the time to wipe up the squeeze-out.

With the cleanup complete on the front half of the boat, it's time to pull the nails in #6, #7, and #8. Then set the jam and repeat the process of coating and applying peanut-butter-thick epoxy.

Figure 13-25

Figure 13-26

Figure 13-27

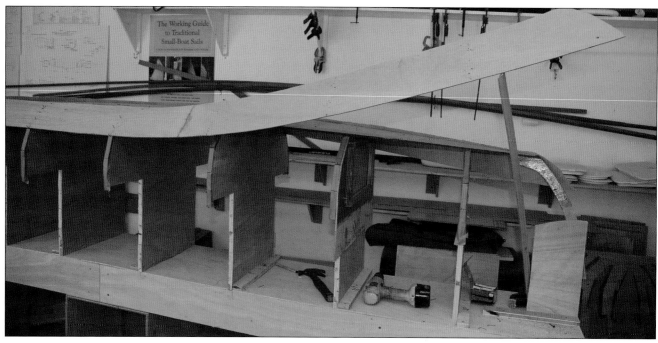

Figure 13-28

Figure 13-29

Figure 13-30

Figure 13-28 shows the jam in place before coating the bottom edge.

This end should go a bit faster than the front half, but cleanup is still very important when you have the back half of the plank nailed in place. In fact there are three important steps after the plank is temporarily nailed down and before the epoxy hardens. Those steps are as follows: Clean up, clean up, and clean up. This one of those boatbuilding details that you will never be sorry you spent extra time taking care of, but you will be very, very sorry if you don't because of the time wasted sanding off the hardened epoxy.

Now that the plank has been epoxied in place and temporarily nailed down it's time to step back and make sure everything is lying fair against the molds and bottom. You may find that there are some gaps between the bottom and garboard that you want to fix. There is an easy way to do this, but care will need to be exercised.

At the point of the gap you'll need to drill a hole that passes through garboard and the bottom, as in **Figure 13-29**. Then set a drywall screw and slowly tighten until the garboard lies against the bottom

(**Figure 13-30**). Here is where you will need to be careful. Just as in **Figure 13-20**, the garboard can be tightened down too much and a hollow put in the plank. Step back and look at the plank from several angles to be sure an unfair hollow isn't there. Sometimes it's better to leave a small gap that can be filled later rather than create a big problem with an unfair spot in the plank.

If you tighten up some gaps or drive an extra nail or two, go back and clean up the squeeze-out. In fact, doing a second wipe-down on inside of the boat would be a good idea anyway. Remember the three steps: Clean up, clean up, and clean up.

When you are certain that all the excess epoxy has been wiped up, then move to the other side of the boat and repeat the process. **Figure 13-31** shows the jam at the bow and the plank ready to be glued

down. This side should be somewhat easier because of the experience you gained on the first side. And when the plank is glued down, temporarily nailed in place, and cleaned up, there is nothing left to do but sit back, wait for the epoxy to cure, and admire how much you've accomplished.

Depending on the temperature, you may have a fairly short time to admire your work. The warmer it is, the faster the epoxy will cure. And once the epoxy has cured, it's time to pull the assembly that held the stem in place because the garboards will now keep the stem from shifting (**Figure 13-32**).

Also in **Figure 13-32**, the bottom and the garboards have been trimmed flush. I have always found a plane to be the best tool for this job. Either a block plane or a bench plane will work, but it will need to be sharpened during the process. Plywood and epoxy are very hard on plane blades.

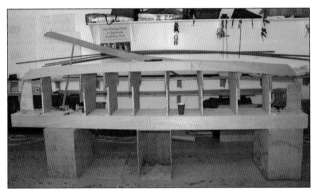

Figure 13-31

Figure 13-32

The next major step, fiberglassing the hull, requires the garboard to be trimmed flush with the bottom and stems. Once trimmed flush, you'll probably discover a number of small gaps; and these will leave a pocket under the fiberglass cloth. **Figure 13-33** shows a small gap where the epoxy didn't quite cover. This and other gaps like it, as well as any nail holes, need to be filled with peanut butter epoxy.

Figure 13-33

Figure 13-34

In **Figure 13-34** any gaps in the stem have been filled, and you can see how the garboard has been rounded over with the plane. Rounding this edge is as important as filling holes and gaps. A very sharp and crisp edge will make it difficult for the cloth to bond well to the plywood. And that can make another potential trouble spot.

In **Figure 13-35** all the gaps and nail holes have been filled, the epoxy has hardened, and the bottom and garboards are ready to be sanded smooth. Having the bottom and planks smooth will make the job of fiberglassing much easier. I like to use 80 grit because it cuts fast and leaves a bit of a tooth on the plywood for a better bond.

When I've finished sanding, I like to sit down about 5 feet in front of the strongback and just to the right of the centerline. With my eye level with or just above the bottom I spend some time just looking. I let my eye flow around the shape of the boat and let my mind wander to the Territory Ahead.

This is one of the real pleasures of boatbuilding. Take the time to sit awhile before moving to the next step.

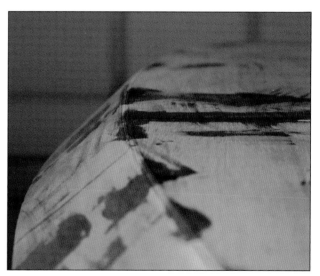

Figure 13-35

14

Putting on the Fiberglass Tape and Cloth

There are several ways to put fiberglass cloth on your boat, and I've used two of them. Interestingly enough both of those ways seem to work equally well. So I'll describe both and give you the reasons why I use each.

The first method I used for a very long time because I thought it had some significant advantages. In some ways I still think that. For a good many years I always pre-coated the boat before I put on the cloth. That is, after I finished sanding the hull, I coated the entire bottom and garboard with epoxy, let it cure, and then sanded it once more before I applied the cloth or fiberglass tape.

The reason I pre-coated the boat was to make sure the cloth or tape didn't get glue-starved. I found that sometimes the wood under the cloth absorbed enough epoxy to create a spot that was almost dry and therefore somewhat weaker. Pre-coating prevents this from happening—but it does come at a price.

Remember in chapter 3 reading about amine blush—that greasy film that appears sometimes as epoxy cures? Well, if there is any amine blush on the hull, the next coat won't bond, so you have to be careful to remove the blush. It's not hard to do:

Wiping the hull down with water and then sanding will eliminate it.

So before I'd put down tape and cloth, I would sand, pre-coat the hull, wipe down plus resand, and then put on the tape and cloth. That's actually somewhat labor intensive and can add at least an extra day, sometimes more depending on the weather.

However, when I teach a class we don't have that extra day, so the tape and cloth are put down over raw wood. Everyone is careful to watch for areas that might be glue-starved, and it works very well. Also, by applying the fiberglass over raw wood the problem of amine blush is eliminated, and a day is saved in the building schedule.

Which method should you use? Well, if you are using an epoxy that doesn't blush, like System Three's SilverTip Laminating Resin, then I say it's a coin toss, but if blush might be an issue then I'd go with putting down the cloth and tape over raw wood.

Because of time considerations I didn't pre-coat Little Princess, even though I used SilverTip Laminating Resin, so we'll proceed with that way.

I like to tape the bottom/garboard seam before I apply the fiberglass cloth. This is where the bottom will take the most beating, so I reinforce it with the fiberglass tape under the cloth. The cloth does add extra weight, a pound or two, and that can add up fast, making a lightweight boat not so lightweight. But I would rather pick up an extra pound or two knowing the boat is good and strong at that point.

So the first step is to measure and cut two strips of fiberglass tape the length of the bottom/garboard seam. The simplest way is to just put it on the boat and cut it to the right length.

I use 3-inch-wide 6-ounce fiberglass tape because it doesn't add much weight. Then, when I apply the 4-ounce fiberglass cloth, there are 10 ounces of cloth over that critical seam.

The 4-ounce tape can be some what difficult to locate, but a search on the internet or one of the suppliers in the appendix should be able to provide it.

Once the tape is cut to the right length, mix up about 6 ounces of resin with the appropriate amount of hardener (from this point on when I give amounts of resin, you can assume I mean it includes the appropriate amount of hardener) and pour the epoxy into a large container. Then take one of the strips and dunk it into the epoxy so it is completely saturated. When you're sure it is completely soaked, use your gloved fingers to squeegee the excess epoxy out of the cloth (**Figure 14-1**) and apply it to the hull (**Figure 14-2**).

Figure 14-1

Figure 14-2

You can stretch the tape a small amount, after several feet are on the hull, to smooth out the wrinkles. Your hand will do a good job of smoothing as well.

After the tape has all the air bubbles and bumps taken out, I like to take a disposable brush and clean up drips and runs. Because this is a very messy process, the last three steps are clean up, clean up, and clean up. You will be very glad you did when it's time to sand.

Do a final check to be sure everything is smooth and all the drips are gone, and then tape the other side. Again, make sure the tape is smooth and bubble-free, do the last three steps and then wait for the epoxy to cure. This will probably take a day depending on the temperature in your shop.

When the epoxy has cured grab your dust mask, some 80-grit sandpaper, and your random orbital sander and start sanding. Notice in **Figure 14-3** that the edge of the boat hasn't been sanded. With light tape like 6-ounce it's very easy to sand right through the material, so care must be taken to not sand away the tape. You just want to feather the rough edges that are visible in **Figure 14-2**.

Because the 80-grit will feather the edges very quickly, you'll be ready to apply the 50-inch-wide 4-ounce fiberglass cloth in short order. Roll out the

Figure 14-3

cloth, smoothing out the wrinkles as you go with your hand. The cloth should be completely smooth and even on the hull. The 50-inch-wide cloth will have extra hanging well below the edge of the garboard, and you'll need to trim this off (**Figure 14-4**).

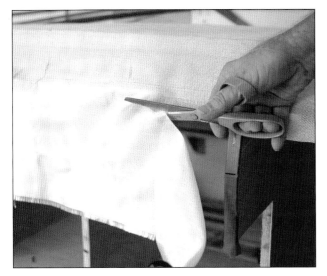

Figure 14-4

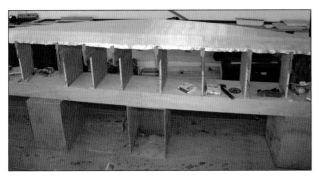

Figure 14-5

In **Figure 14-5** masking tape has been used to hold the trimmed cloth on the hull. It never fails that a small puff or big gust of wind comes along just as you start to pour epoxy on the cloth. If the cloth isn't taped in place, this will cause a problem.

You can also eliminate another potential problem by cutting a dart in the cloth at the bow and stern (**Figure 14-6**). Start by making a cut on centerline, and then remove a small triangle of cloth on both sides of the centerline. This will allow the cloth to lie flat against the garboard as the epoxy is

applied. If you don't cut the dart, the weight of the wet cloth tends to pull it away from the garboard.

With the darts cut and the cloth taped down, take about 8 ounces of resin, mixed for about 90 seconds, and pour it down the center of the bottom. Using a squeegee spread the epoxy over the bottom and then work the epoxy down the garboards (**Figure 14-7**). The squeegee in **14-7** was made from a scrap piece of 4mm plywood with the edges sanded smooth. Whatever you use as a squeegee should have all rough edges removed. A rough edge can hang on the cloth and make it difficult to spread the epoxy puddles. You'll want to spread the puddles over the bottom and then work small amounts to the garboards. Pulling a big puddle down the side will result in most going onto the floor rather than into the cloth.

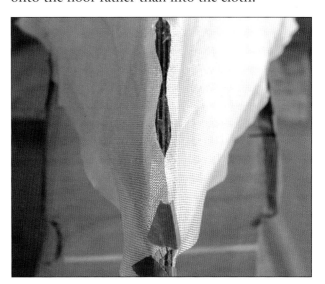

Figure 14-6

Figure 14-7

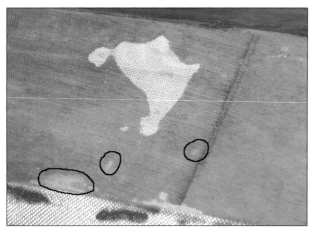
Figure 14-8

In **Figure 14-9** all the bubbles have been pressed out, the areas around the bow and stern have been worked over, and the epoxy is curing. Notice all the epoxy on the plywood sheets on the floor—that is why I recommend using plywood under the boat.

Once the epoxy has cured but is still a bit soft or green, trim the cloth flush with the edge of the garboard. I use a single-edge razor blade for this job, but a box knife will work too (**Figure 14-10**). You'll find green epoxy much easier to cut than fully cured epoxy.

This is another time I like to sit in that special spot just off the bow. The epoxy hasn't fully cured and it's a good time for a breather to assess just how far you've progressed.

Where the epoxy doesn't absorb into the cloth will be white spots like **Figure 14-8**. The large white spots are easy to see, but you need to look for the bubbles and areas where the cloth is wet but not down on the wood. In **Figure 14-8** some of the harder-to-see bubbles have circles drawn around them. Learn to look for these as well as the large dry spots.

I've found that many times the best way to deal with these bubbles is to press them down with your gloved hand. Using your hands as a squeegee works well, and that's why I always wear two pair of gloves instead of one when fiberglassing. The two gloves are just added protection when working with areas like the bow and stern.

Figure 14-10

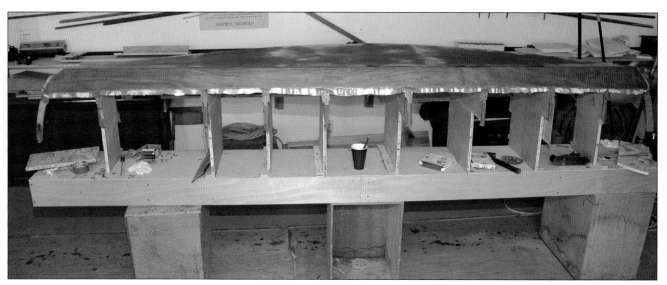
Figure 14-9

15

Beveling the Garboards and Hanging the Mid-Planks

Figure 15-1

Figure 15-2

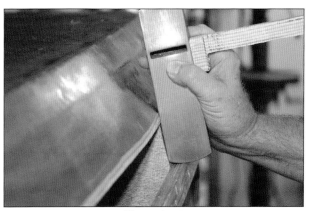
Figure 15-3

Figure 15-4

Beveling the garboard is really just like beveling the bottom. The only difference is that the garboard is covered with fiberglass cloth and that will make planing a bevel slightly more difficult because the cloth is tougher to cut through. It also means you'll have to sharpen the plane blade a few times during the process.

So when your plane is good and sharp, screw down the batten between the edge of the garboard and the upper chine as in **Figure 15-1** and start cutting the bevel (**Figure 15-2**). You'll want to continue to plane the bevel until your plane fits against each station mold with little or no gap (**Figure 15-3**).

It is possible to continue to plane down past the inside layer of plywood, and you want to avoid this. **Figure 15-4** is a close-up of plywood beveled down to the inside layer. The edge is still intact, and the line of the plank is continuous. In **Figure 15-5** the bevel has continued through the inside layer, and the line of the plank is broken and ragged. This can be avoided by not making your cuts too aggressive and keeping the downward pressure on the plane to a minimum.

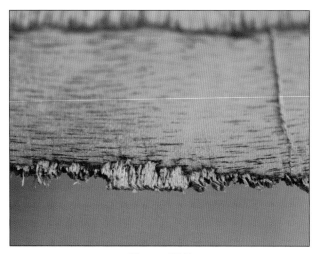

Figure 15-5

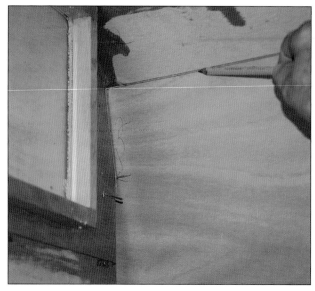

Figure 15-7

Also, you'll want to stop the planing the bevel about halfway between Station #1 and where the garboard meets the stem. Do this between #8 and the stem as well. Once the mid-plank is up on the strongback, you'll finish the bevel out by cutting a gain. We'll get to cutting gains a little later in the next chapter.

Figure 15-6 shows the blank for the mid-plank up on the strongback and ready to be marked and rough-cut. You'll do this much like you did the garboard—but there are a few differences.

In **Figure 15-7** the upper chine has been clearly marked and a line drawn along the bottom edge of the garboard, much like the line you drew along the garboard where it met the bottom. Notice that

a line has been put on each side of the mold, and the station number written by the mold. When this has been done at each station, pull the blank off and lay it on a flat surface.

Now connect all the marks you made at the upper chine of each station, just like you did with the lower chine on the garboard and just like in **Figure 15-8**. Once all those points are connected and you have the line for the upper chine, pull off the batten and set it aside for a moment.

At this point the blank has a line for the upper chine, which you just struck, and a line for the lower chine, which you drew while the blank was

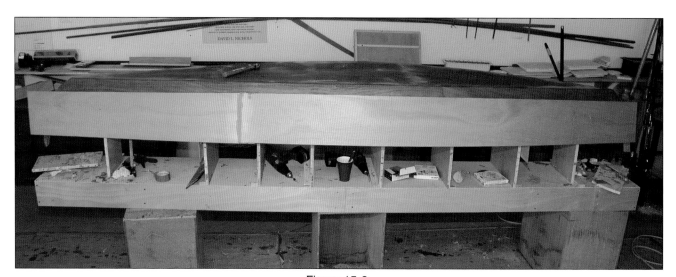

Figure 15-6

Figure 15-8

Figure 15-9

Figure 15-10

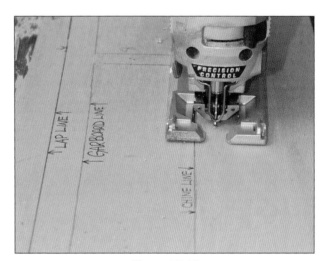

Figure 15-11

on the strongback. But you also need a line for the lap, which extends up from the lower chine line. So at each station, measure up 1 inch from the lower chine, place a mark (**Figure 15-9**), and then, using the batten to connect them, strike a line (**Figure 15-10**).

Next, cut about an inch outside the chine line (**Figure 15-11**), about an inch outside the lap line

Figure 15-12

Figure 15-13

Figure 15-14

Figure 15-15

Figure 15-16

(**Figure 15-12**), and put the rough-cut plank back on the strongback (**Figure 15-13**).

The rough-cut plank should match up with the line once it's up on the strongback (**Figure 15-14**), and there needs to be at least an inch of lap extending above the garboard. This will be very important at the bow and stern (**Figure 15-15**). Of course, just like with the garboard, this plank needs to lie against each station mold and should be touching the garboard along its entire length.

It may take a bit of adjustment so the plank lines up where it should, and this may cause the plank to be off the original marks, as in **Figure 15-16**. This correction still leaves enough lap at the stern (**Figure 15-17**), so note the new marks and pull the rough-cut plank off for the final cut.

When the new lines have been struck, cut just outside the chine and lap line, then plane down to the final shape (**Figures 15-18** and **15-19**). Again,

Figure 15-17

Figure 15-18

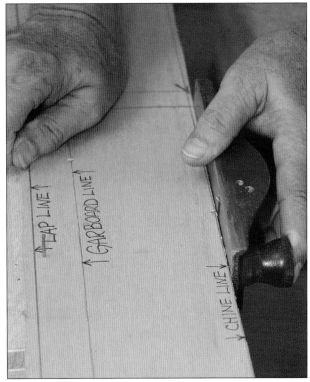

Figure 15-19

Figure 15-20

the block plane will work best for this job, and I find that using a shallow or non-aggressive cut gives a very smooth, even line.

It will be a good idea to try to get both edges of the plank as smooth as possible before you put on the strongback. Once it's back on the molds and every mark is matched up, you'll want to put the registration nails at the chine line and mark the

plank with an arrow and station number (**Figure 15-20**). Do this at every station, just like you did for the garboard.

And just like you did for the garboard, pull this plank and move it to the other side of the boat to see how well it matches. It may take slight movement fore or aft and small adjustments up and down to get a good fit. It will be easiest if you start at #5 and make adjustments from there. If every-

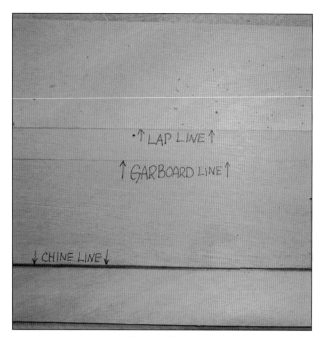

Figure 15-21

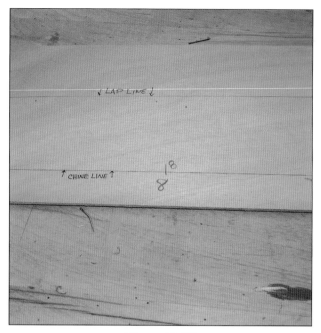

Figure 15-22

thing matches and fits well, and it should, then you can use the plank as a pattern for this side.

Pull this plank off and nail it on the other mid-plank blank so it can be used as a pattern. Trace the outline of the plank and make notes at each station (**Figure 15-21**). Be sure to transfer the information inside the lines so those reference points won't be cut off (**Figure 15-22**). Cut just proud of the line (just outside the line) and use the plane to get the final shape.

Now put both planks on their respective sides and step back a bit. These planks won't come off again, and the boat is really starting to flesh out. Sit down in that sweet spot and let your mind float downstream, to the Territory Ahead. Personally, I think the time spent thinking about all the places the boat will carry you, all the adventures that lie in the future, is integral to boatbuilding and to life. So enjoy a few moments in the future and admire what you have accomplished so far.

16

Cutting the Gains and Gluing Up the Mid-Planks

With the two mid-planks on the boat, you may find that no matter how you adjusted the planks, the lap edges refused to line up (**Figure 16-1**). Obviously you want the plank ends to match at the bow and the stern, so you'll need to plane down the higher lap until it is level with the lower one (**Figures 16-2** and **16-3**).

Figure 16-2

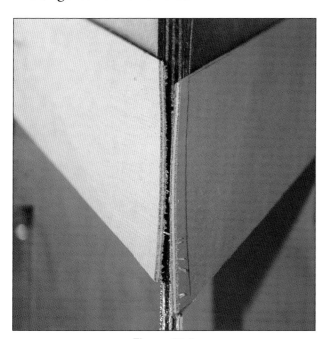
Figure 16-1

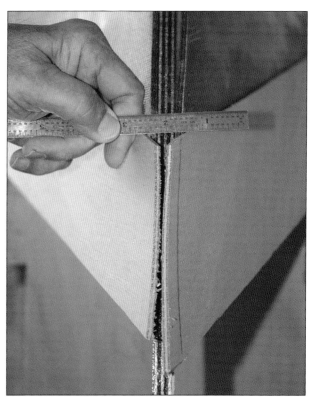
Figure 16-3

In **Figure 16**-4 the planks match, but there is a large gap created by the overlap. Cutting the gain will eliminate this gap; the plank will lie tight against the stem and be flush with the garboard.

Figure 16-4

I don't know why it is called cutting a gain, because what you are really doing is inletting the mid-plank into the garboard or the plank above into the plank below.

It took awhile for me to figure out gains. I'm not sure why, really, because it's not that hard to do. I tried several different ways and finally settled on the method I use now.

The top of the mid-plank acts as the guide for the first cut, and because the plank stays on the boat, getting it to drop back in the exact spot isn't a problem. Once the first cut is made, the mid-plank is gently bent back and held in place with a jam, just like epoxying the garboard.

Figure 16-5 shows using the corner of a sharp chisel to cut the line along the top of the plank (it's not really the top of the plank—the boat is upside down—but visually it's the top of the plank). You'll want to start the cut about 10 inches back from the stem, making it shallow at the start and deep at the stem. Don't try to do it in one pass with the chisel; use multiple passes and work carefully. The single white line is the result of a wayward cut and careless moment.

Figure 16-5

Figure 16-6

When the groove is well defined, then use a rabbet plane or chisel to start cutting the gain. **Figure 16-6** shows a rabbet plane starting to cut the gain. I like to use a rabbet plane because the sharp corner of the plane fits nicely in the groove made by the chisel. Notice in **Figure 16-6** that the V channel made by the rabbet plane is well defined and deep.

Once the V groove is well established, then start planing the slope toward the stem (**Figure 16-7**).

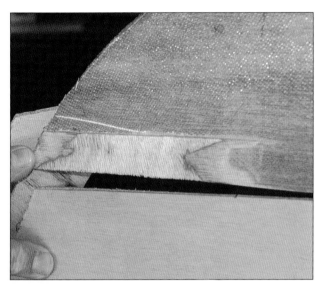

Figure 16-7

Figure 16-8

One of the problems with the rabbet plane is that it leaves a small ridge under the cut made by the chisel. The best way to square up that groove is with a sharp chisel (**Figure 16-8**).

The goal is to cut a wedge that removes almost the entire plank at the stem and then tapers back toward Station #1 (**Figure 16-9**). The depth of the cut at the stem should be equal to or almost equal to the thickness of the plank that will fit in the gain. That way the surface of, in this case, the mid-plank will be flush with the surface of the garboard (**Figure 16-10**). Now just repeat the process for the other side and for the stern (**Figure 16-11**).

Figure 16-9

Figure 16-10

The most difficult problem you should have is working around the mid-plank or the plank you're cutting the gain for. Just remember to treat the planks gently and try not to put sharp bends in

Figure 16-11

Figure 16-12

Figure 16-13

them. Actually, a wedge like the one shown in **Figure 16-12** will hold the plank out way from the hull and simplify not only cutting the gains but also applying the epoxy. All the nails up to and including #5 have been pulled, and two have been driven in molds #6, #7, and #8. This is the same way you applied the epoxy to the garboard; these tasks will become more repetitive as construction on the boat progresses.

Applying epoxy to the raw edge of the bevel on the garboard is a familiar job at this point (**Figure 16-13**). However, don't forget to coat the top edge of the mid-plank as well. Once the bevel and the top edge of the plank are coated to a point just beyond #5, you should apply the peanut-butter-thick epoxy. As you work forward, be sure to leave a space at each station mold for easy cleanup (**Figure 16-14**), and liberally coat the gain and the stem (**Figure 16-15**).

Figure 16-14

With everything coated, remove the jam and work from #5 toward the bow. Having the plank resting on the registration nails will help make sure everything is lined up as you move forward. It may be better to set a single nail in #5 and #4 and then jump forward to the bow to set a single nail there. Sometimes a gentle tug right before you set the nail at the bow will pull everything in tight. Be sure that the plank sits tight against the garboard in the gain before you set the temporary nail. Then go back and finish temporarily-nailing #3, #2, and #1.

You'll want to come back to the bow once the front half of the plank is down and in place. I like to set two drywall screws to pull the plank down tight against the stem. Generally I find that I need to set a temporary nail right at the top of the gain to make sure the surfaces of the two planks stay flush (**Figure 16-16**). Then come the last three steps before you epoxy the back half. Remember to clean up, clean up, and then clean up.

From this point on everything is familiar territory as you finish gluing up both mid-planks (**Figure 16-17**). It will be a good idea, once you have finished, to walk around the boat and make sure the planks are tight against the hull and molds. As you check, take pride in what you've done and the skills you've acquired.

Figure 16-15

Figure 16-16

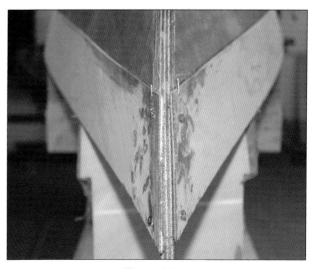
Figure 16-17

17

Putting on the Sheer Planks

Figure 17-2

Putting on the sheer plank is really just a repetition of what you have done with the mid-plank and garboard. And what that means is that at this point in the construction process, you have a good knowledge and skill base. So, there's nothing new here, just a couple of tips to make the job a little easier.

Figure 17-1 shows what I have come to call Hanging Helpers. Hanging Helpers are a refinement of a method I used to capture the plank and were created by one of my students at Wooden-Boat School. He took one look at what I was doing, grabbed some scrap plywood, and knocked out a bunch of Hanging Helpers.

One look at Figure 17-2 and you can see why you would need something to help capture the sheer blank. The bottom edge extends far below the molds, making it difficult to handle, particularly for one person. But the Hanging Helpers hold the blank and are easily adjustable while you position it and get it temporarily nailed in place.

Figure 17-3 shows a close-up view of the inside of the plank. To adjust the height, loosen the spring clamp slightly and raise or lower the blank. This allows for small movements until you are happy with the rough fit. Then starting at #5, temporarily nail it in place while you draw the continuous chine line and mark the sheer at each mold.

In Figure 17-4, just like with the mid-plank, both the sheer and the lap line have been drawn

Figure 17-1

Figure 17-3

Figure 17-5

Figure 17-4

Figure 17-6

using a batten. I like to make the sheer lap just a little larger, about ¼ inch bigger, than the mid-plank lap, because this gives me a bit more adjustment. You may want to make the lap about 1½ inches for just a little extra wiggle room. You can always plane it off if it's not needed. Also, cutting about 1½ inches outside the sheer line will give you more latitude when you set the sheer line.

That latitude can be welcome if you find in the final fit that the sheer plank only overlaps the mid-plank by ½ inch or less. A ½-inch overlap will work, of course, but ¾ to 1 inch is better.

So make the lap 1½ inches, cut just proud of the lap line (**Figure 17-5**), and then plane down to the line with a block plane (**Figure 17-6**). Remember to use a shallow, non-aggressive cut once you

Figure 17-7

reach the line. This will give a very nice smooth line before the plank is temporarily nailed back up for a trial fit.

In **Figure 17-7** the plank has been put back on the boat for a trial fit. If the chine line matches the chine of the mid-plank, the sheer line matches the sheer on the molds, and the plank fits tightly against the hull, then you can move to the next step. However, you may find that some slight adjustment is in order for a good fit. Moving the plank as little as ½ inch can sometimes make the difference between an acceptable fit and a very good fit. On occasion I have had to adjust a plank back and forth for 15 or 20 minutes to get it to fit just right. If it doesn't work the first few times, keep playing with it until you hit that "just right" spot.

A close look at Stations #3, #4, #5, and #6 in **Figure 17-7** shows the Hanging Helpers still in use. Keeping these in place until the sheer plank is nailed in place for the final time will make fine-tuning the adjustments much easier.

When you find that "just right" spot, set two nails at each station and measure the width of the mid-plank at Station #5. In **Figure 17-8** the mid-plank measures 3¾ inches from the lap of the sheer plank to the lap of the mid-plank. This is an arbitrary number and could just as easily be 4 inches or 3½ inches. For example, if there had been more than an inch overlap at #5 I would have planed it down so there was ¾- to 1-inch overlap. Use whatever measurement seems to work best. But regardless of the measurement, there should be at least ½

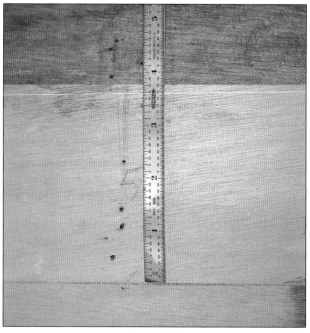

Figure 17-8

Figure 17-9

inch overlap at Station #5.

Take the measurement of the mid-plank at Station #5, in this case 3¾ inches, and mark the sheer plank at #4, #3, #2, and #1 as well as the bow (**Figure 17-9**). Then do the same toward the stern (**Figure 17-10**).

At this juncture you have two choices: Plane the

Figure 17-10

Figure 17-12

Figure 17-11

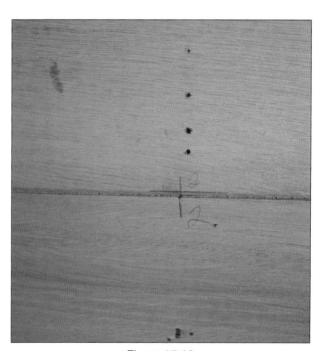

Figure 17-13

plank on the boat or remove it and draw the line with a batten. If the plank popped right up and dropped in place for a perfect fit, then I'd pull it and strike the line with the batten. However, if the plank was a struggle to fit or has just a small amount to plane off, I'd plane it on the boat. If you're going to plane the plank on the boat, it

might be a good idea to put some tick marks between the stations. Those tick marks can act as a guide while planing down. In **Figure 17-11** the plank was left on the boat because there was only a maximum of an inch to take off.

The main things to remember are to take your time, don't make aggressive cuts, and step back to check the progress so you plane a sweeping fair line. Making long continuous cuts will also help prevent planing a hollow in the line.

Once a sweeping line has been achieved, put registration marks at each station (**Figure 17-12**). **Figure 17-13** is a close-up of the registration mark at Station #2. Be sure to get the horizontal line right at the top of the sheer plank and carry the vertical line across the edge of the plank. That way it will be possible to replace this plank in almost the exact same spot. I like to tack-nail the Hanging Helpers so they fix the vertical height as well. Then they serve somewhat the same function as the registration nails on the mid-plank and garboard.

There is one other step that will make moving this plank to the other side easier. Transfer the width of the mid-plank at Station #5 to the other mid-plank. Measure down from the lap line 3¾ inches, or whatever dimension you used, and put a tick mark. Do this at each station and the tick marks will provide an accurate starting point for the plank. And don't forget to have Hanging Helpers on the other side as well.

Moving this plank to the opposite side is no different from moving the mid-plank or garboard. It may or may not match exactly with the stations or the height tick marks, but it should be very close. Once you're sure it will fit the way you want, pull it, use it as a pattern (just like the mid-plank and garboard), cut it out, and put it on the boat.

What do you do if it didn't match up the way you wanted? It's easy, really: Just make notes where it falls short and then increase the width of the plank at those points. Cut it a little proud, put it back on the boat for the final fit, and then trim it to shape.

When both planks are in place on the boat, you'll want to measure the width of the mid-plank on each side of the station line to be sure the it's the same on both sides at that station. Basically it's what you did in **Figures 17-8** and **17-9**. They don't

have to be exactly the same—just close enough that they look equal when you look at the boat from the bow or stern (**Figure 17-14**). **Figure 17-15** is a close-up of the bow and shows that the ends of the sheer plank are equal.

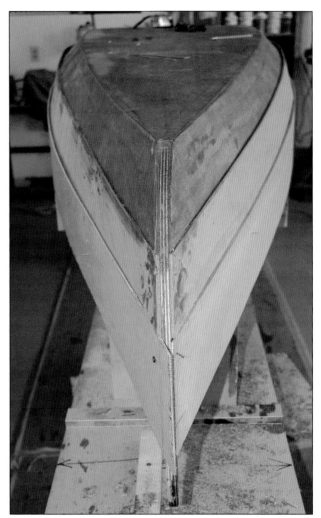

Figure 17-14

Figure 17-15

At this point, like both the mid-plank and garboard, these planks won't come off the boat again and are ready to be epoxied in place. This is the same procedure as before: Just remove the nails back to #5, put in the jam, and epoxy.

Figure 17-16 shows the boat with both planks glued on and the boat planked in. In my shop I always consider this a big moment because with the sheer planks glued in place, it's officially a boat. It's not finished, of course, but there aren't any more planks to put on and there is nothing left to imagine about the shape of the hull. In fact, in the water it would float—with a few slow leaks, I suspect, but you could paddle it.

I always congratulate my students when they get this far because of all they have learned and accomplished. So kick back and admire what you've accomplished and how far you've come.

The Territory Ahead is much closer.

Figure 17-16

18

The Work Before Turn-Over

Even though the boat is now planked in, there is still some work to be done before it will be ready to pull off the strongback and turn over. I've found that doing these tasks in a particular order will expedite the process, because you're not waiting for epoxy to dry in order to proceed.

The first order of business is to make some deck beams. You won't need these until later, but making them now will assure they are ready when you need them. Nothing is more frustrating than being delayed by the lack of a part or piece of hardware.

So to not be delayed, find some scrap 4mm plywood and rip five strips 1½ inches wide by approximately 24 inches long. Then rip five strips 3 inches wide by approximately 24 inches long. Next, tack the 1½ inch strips to a flat surface and put a small amount of peanut butter epoxy on one long edge of the 3-inch-wide strip, then set it in the center of 1½-inch strip. Small finish nails will help hold the 3-inch piece upright while the epoxy cures (**Figure 18-1**). This will give you the four deck beams you'll need—with one spare, just in case.

Now move from making deck beams to under the boat and put a mark at each station at the sheer along with that mark's station number. This mark can be used to transfer the sheer line to the outside of the plank if needed.

Also, it's important that the bulkheads be epoxied to the boat—but use just a small amount, more of a tab or tack. The goal is to just hold it in place so the bulkhead provides some support but not with large amounts of epoxy.

For my first few boats I used large amounts of epoxy, but because I was working under the boat

Figure 18-1

(so to speak) it was hard to reach, and the job was always messy. That always made for extra sanding and work later. So I started using small amounts of epoxy and wiped up any excess carefully. I found that taking a small amount of peanut butter epoxy on my finger and wiping it along the joint would push enough epoxy between the bulkhead and plank to hold securely. And then I always followed the last three steps and cleaned up, cleaned up, and cleaned up (**Figure 18-2**).

Figure 18-3

Figure 18-2

While the epoxy is curing inside the boat, turn your attention to the bottom and garboard. It's time to fill the weave in the fiberglass cloth. This isn't just for cosmetics. Running a finger across the bottom demonstrates how rough the surface really is. That rough surface will create drag in the water. You want the boat to slip though the water with as little resistance as possible, but epoxy adds weight to the boat. The trick is to add just enough to fill the weave and no more.

In **Figure 18-3** the right side of the bottom has been brushed with unthickened epoxy; the left side is dry. By looking at the hull at different angles you'll be able to see when the weave has been filled. Start at one end and slowly work your way to the other. If you maintain a line (**Figure 18-3**), it will be easy to keep track of where you have applied the epoxy. Pouring and spreading the epoxy, like put-

Figure 18-4

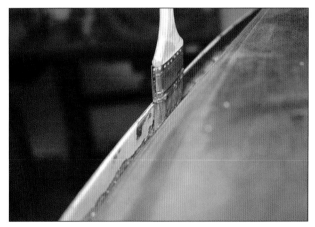
Figure 18-5

ting on the cloth, might be faster, but will add too much epoxy and weight. I like to use a disposable brush for this job even though it will leave a few bristles. Let the epoxy cure and then sand with 80-grit paper (**Figure 18-4**).

While you're waiting for the epoxy to cure, take what's left of the unthickened epoxy and coat the inside of all the laps (**Figure 18-5**). This will help the

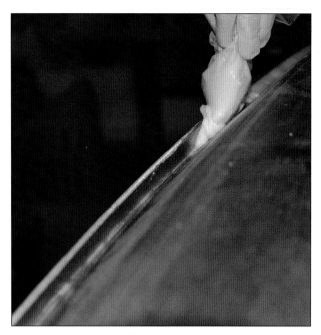

Figure 18-6

Figure 18-7

thickened epoxy get a good bond. That's important, because the filled laps provide structural strength. Then fill a baggie with peanut butter epoxy and basically inject the thickened epoxy into the lap (**Figure 18-6**). Cut about a 1/8-inch-wide hole in one corner of the baggie so it acts like a pastry bag used to decorate cakes. The goal is to fill the lap completely level with the thick epoxy, and the baggie makes a fast job of getting the epoxy into the lap.

Another fast way to completely fill the laps is using System Three's SilverTip nonsagging adhesive. With the tube there is no mixing—just apply with the caulking gun and it's mixed in the nozzle (**Figure 18-7**). I did find that the more expensive caulking gun with some compound leverage made the job easier. Also, if you use the nonsagging adhesive, don't pre-coat the lap with epoxy—or else be sure it has cured before using it.

And while the epoxy in the laps is curing, you can work on all those holes created by the temporary nails and any other flaws in the planks. When I first started, I filled those holes with thickened epoxy, but the epoxy is so much harder than the wood that sanding proved to be a problem. I switched to microballoons mixed with epoxy and found this better but still too hard. I even tried Bondo, used by auto shops. This sanded fairly well but I occasionally had some issues with it adhering to the epoxy, so I went back to microballoons and epoxy.

Then System Three came out with QuikFair and now that's what I use. QuikFair is the same hardness as the wood so it sands easily and smooth. It mixes into a heavy nonsagging paste that stays where I put it and has a fairly long pot life. So when I got careless and created a fairly large trough with the sander, that's what I reached for.

In **Figure 18-8** a heavy coat of fairing compound, in this case QuikFair, has been applied to

Figure 18-8

the problem plank. Be sure that there is plenty of fairing compound, whatever you use, on either side of the area to be filled.

Use the time waiting for the fairing compound to harden by making a longboard. A longboard is nothing more than a flexible board with handles and sandpaper on the bottom (**Figure 18-9**). The longboard in **Figure 18-9** is a 4-inch-wide by 20-inch-long piece of 9mm scrap (but 6mm would have been better). A 4 x 24 coarse sanding belt has been stapled to the board and handles cut from ¾-inch scrap.

Figure 18-9

Figure 18-10

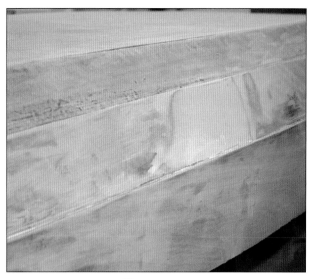

Figure 18-11

Figure 18-12

In **Figure 18-10** the longboard is being used to sand the filled area on the plank. Because the board is longer than the filled area, it will sand it level with the plank on either side. In **Figure 18-11** sanding is complete; however, a close inspection will reveal some pinholes that will need to be filled and resanded with the longboard.

To make good use of the filler, those pinholes can be filled at the same time all the nail holes are filled. Go over the boat carefully and try to fill every nail hole. A small amount of filler on a putty knife works very well. In **Figure 18-12** the nail holes have been filled; in **Figure 18-13** they have been sanded down, and the boat is ready for an overall coat of epoxy.

Figure 18-13

Coating the entire hull with epoxy (**Figure 18-14**) has two benefits: It gives whatever finish you are going to use a consistent base, and it gives the wood a barrier against water.

With that final coat of epoxy, the boat is ready to come off the strongback and be turned over. This means that the strongback can be disassembled and stored for future boats, and the car can be moved back in from the driveway. The boat can be put on pulleys above the car or in the backyard on sawhorses to be worked on in the evenings or weekends. Maybe just leave the car in the driveway a bit longer—the boat is so hard to admire on pulleys or covered up in the backyard.

Figure 18-14

19

Setting the Sheer

When the epoxy has cured, the big moment of pulling the boat off the strongback and turning it over has arrived. I've turned boats over by myself, but it is really a job for two people. It doesn't take a great deal of strength—just another pair of hands.

To prepare for the big moment, crawl under the boat and pull all the nails in both bulkheads. It may take a pair of pliers to reach those hard-to-get nails, but run your hand over the bulkhead to be sure you have pulled each one. It's easy to leave one behind.

With all the nails pulled, lift the bow, right at the stem, until it breaks loose. If you're picking up the strongback, then either there is still a nail in a bulkhead or a mold has been glued to the hull. Generally you should be able to see what is keeping the boat stuck. But if there isn't a nail and you can't find which mold has attached itself to the boat, don't panic; there is a solution. Starting with #5, unscrew the mold from the cleat and push the bottom away from the cleat. This will break #5 free, and you can remove the mold. Do this until you find the attached mold. Don't try to break it loose; just unscrew the mold from the cleat then the boat will break free and lift off.

Now with the boat turned over, it's easy to see where the mold is attached and easy to free it from the boat. In **Figure 19-1** the boat has all the molds removed and is ready to set the sheer.

You have two choices at this point: You can use the sheer line from the plans, or you can set the line yourself. I find I rarely use the sheer line from the plans (the marks you made right before turn-over). I set it myself.

In **Figure 19-2** the 5/8 x ¾-inch outwale has been clamped on the boat at sheer line from the plans (the line you struck on the sheer plank) and will be adjusted from there.

I like to stand back and look at the sheer line from as many angles as possible. I may move the outwale down at #5 a small amount and up at the bow and stern, look at that, and then make more

Figure 19-1

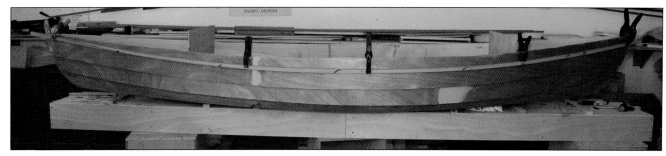

Figure 19-2

adjustments until I'm satisfied with the line.

This is something that is a matter of personal taste, so take your time and find exactly the right line for your eye. Once you look at the outwale and feel that's exactly the right spot, set a series of 6 x 5/8-inch screws about 8 inches apart (**Figure 19-3**). These screws are set from the inside into the outwale, and it will be a good idea to pre-drill each screw.

Figure 19-3

Figure 19-4

Sometimes setting a screw at a point of high stress in the outwale can cause a problem, even with pre-drilling. In **Figure 19-4** the hole weakened the outwale enough to break. This can be caused by an existing weak spot—or, in the case of **Figure 19-4** the screw can cause the break. In either case replace the broken outwale and skip that screw.

Note the small hole right above the outwale in **Figure 19-4**. That hole was used to transfer the sheer line on the line to the outside. Remember the marks you made at the sheer line of each mold? A hole was drilled at each of those marks, and the top edge of the outwale was sprung to match them.

The next step is to transfer the line of this outwale to the other side. To do this, at each station measure up from the lap to the bottom of the outwale (**Figure 19-5**) and make a note of the measurement. Now move to the other side of the station

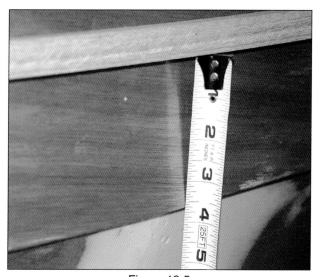

Figure 19-5

Figure 19-6

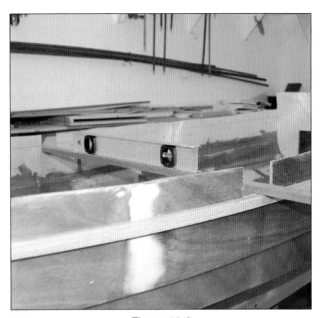

Figure 19-8

Figure 19-7

Figure 19-9

and transfer that distance to the sheer plank. Doing this at each station gives a series of marks that you can spring the outwale to, just like a batten. Starting at #5, clamp the bottom of the outwale just at the mark and then move to each station in turn.

When both the outwales are in place, you'll want to check to see if they are level. First drill a small hole at the top of the outwale on both sides at #2 and #7. **Figure 19-6** and **Figure 19-7** show the hole for #2. **Figure 19-7** indicates that the out-

wale is slightly higher on that side, so it was pushed down until it matched the other side.

To check for level amidships, saw a small section out and span the width of the boat with a straight board in the slot. Make sure the bottom is level athwartship and then check the span for level (**Figure 19-8**). If it is only 1/16 to an 1/8 inch out of level, you shouldn't worry too much—it may create bigger problems by getting it perfectly level. If it's ½ inch or more (which it shouldn't be),

Figure 19-10

then you should move the high side down until
the sheer line and the outwales appear even and
level (**Figure 19-9**). Then take the Japanese saw
and trim off the excess plank down to the top of
the outwale (**Figure 19-10**).

20

Fillet and Tape

With the sheer line set, you now need to fillet and tape the bulkheads and the bottom/garboard joint. Compared with what you've done so far, this is very easy. In fact you've already taped the outside of the bottom/garboard, so this is really just a repeat of jobs you already know how to do.

Before you get started on these jobs and after you pre-measure the tape for the bottom/garboard joint, make yourself a couple of tools. The first tool will help put a nice even fillet between the bulkhead and the hull (**Figure 20-1**); the second is used for the bottom/garboard joint (**Figure 20-2**). The bulkhead tool is about 4 inches by 3 inches and has a 7/8-inch notch cut off one end. The bottom/garboard tool starts with a square about the same size, but then the angle of the bottom and garboard joint is transferred to the square and a notch 1 inch wide is cut off the corner.

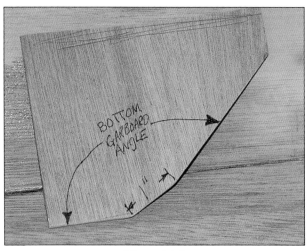

Figure 20-2

Set these tools to one side while you mix up some peanut butter epoxy. Start with about 6 ounces of resin, add the thickener, and load a baggie with a small notch cut out of the corner. Also, if you are going to varnish your boat instead of painting, it will be important to mix some wood flour into the peanut butter epoxy to give it a wood color.

This is just like in Chapter 18. Those familiar with a pastry bag will see some similarities in the use of the baggie and pastry bag.

The baggie can put a large amount of epoxy right where the bulkhead joins the hull. Start just past the centerline of the bottom and run a continuous bead of peanut butter epoxy (**Figure 20-3**) along the joint.

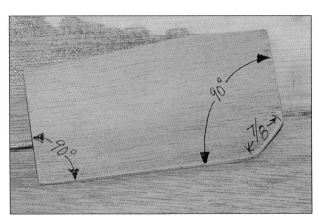

Figure 20-1

Figure 20-3

Figure 20-4

Figure 20-5

Figure 20-6

Hold the fillet tool as in **Figure 20-4** and keep it pushed against the bottom and bulkhead. Then with a continuous dragging motion, spread a smooth even bead of epoxy. Pick up any excess epoxy with the tool and then wipe the bottom and bulkhead clean. Be careful not to wipe the bead and clean out the area right at the sheer (**Figure 20-5**). This is where the inwale will fit against the bulkhead, and it will be easier to install if that spot is free of epoxy (**Figure 20-6**). Repeat this process for the other side and for both sides of the other bulkhead.

In the process of putting fillets on the bulkheads, there will left over peanut butter in the baggies. Don't throw that extra away; squeeze it next to the bow and stern stems (**Figure 20-7**). Smooth it out and continue to work. If the entire length of the stem isn't covered on both sides, mix up a little more and finish the job. It's very important to put a fillet where the stem meets the bottom. In **Figure 20-7** the fillet needs to cover that area. I find it isn't necessary to mix much to finish the job. There always seems to be enough extra, particularly when doing the bottom/garboard sections.

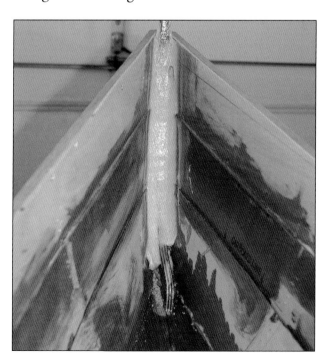

Figure 20-7

Figure 20-8

Figure 20-10

Figure 20-9

Figure 20-11

In **Figure 20-8** the bottom/garboard joint has been coated with unthickened epoxy, and a bead of mayonnaise-thick epoxy has been run along the entire length of the cockpit. You want to use a softer, more easily spread epoxy under the tape because it gives a smoother seam.

Use the bottom fillet tool and smooth out the bead (**Figure 20-9**). Then take the precut length of 6-ounce tape, dunk it in the bucket of epoxy, and squeegee it with your double-gloved fingers (**Figure 20-10**). Roll up the tape as you squeegee; this will make the dripping wet tape easier to handle. Now,

starting at one bulkhead, roll out about half the tape over the soft epoxy (**Figure 20-11**) and then go back to smooth out the tape into the epoxy. Having the epoxy soft allows the thickened epoxy to work into the weave of the tape; I think this makes for a stronger bond. You'll want to work out any air bubbles also. As you get to the end of the tape, pull and smooth with your hand (**Figure 20-12**). This will help force out any air bubbles and create a nice even surface that should have the appearance of **Figure 20-13**. Now do the other side of the cockpit and then move to the area inside the compartments.

Figure 20-12

Figure 20-13

The interior of the compartment won't show, and I never spend much time being neat and tidy in places that don't show. It is important to not have sharp points of epoxy or strands of tape; these will snag and tear gear stored in the compartments. Other than that, don't worry about appearance—unless you want to, of course.

Generally, about the time I finish taping both sides of the cockpit, the epoxy fillets on the bulkheads are firm but still soft. In hot weather, this will happen much quicker, so I check as I work. When it reaches that firm but still soft texture, I take a disposable brush and unthickened epoxy and brush the fillets. Taking care to not press too hard, I can brush the fillets to a glassy smooth surface.

I have also used a curved cabinet scraper to put a slight cove or curve in the fillet. This is done when the epoxy is hardened but still green—that is, the epoxy hasn't reached full hardness yet. But if you are careful with the fillet tool, when you first do the fillet not much scraping or sanding will be necessary.

At this point you can do the interior side of the bulkhead, but I like to wait until the outside fillet is hard. That way there isn't any danger of disturbing the outside fillet. The main thing to remember is to take your time and enjoy the process. If you mess up a fillet, just scrape it out, wipe it down and start over. Just remember to enjoy.

21

Deck Beams and Sheer Clamps

The decks of all three of these canoes have a camber. That is, these decks have a curve, a convex curve. This has several purposes like: shedding water quickly, reserve buoyancy, and—probably the most important reason—appearance.

Over the years I've increased the camber and decreased the camber, looking for the best appearance, and have found that 2½ inches to 2¾ inches of camber looks the best to my eye. So the canoes

in this book have decks with a 2½-inch camber.

Exactly how do you go about building decks with a 2½-inch camber—or any camber, for that matter? Fortunately I ran across an article early in my boatbuilding that showed how to make a jig that would strike a curve on a deck beam. And more importantly, each beam would be consistent as the boat's beam narrowed.

In **Figure 21-1**, a baseline has been drawn, and points A, B, and C have been marked on it. I like to work on a large piece of plywood on my worktable, but putting the ply on the floor would work just as well. Points A and C are the maximum beam of the boat at the bulkhead, in this case 24 inches, and point B is the centerline of the beam. A perpendicular line has been drawn up from B and a point 2½ inches up marked at point B'.

Next set a nail at A, C, and B' and position the arms of the jig so they touch the nails. Then set a butt plate (a piece of plywood to connect the two arms) to connect the two arms and you're ready to mark some deck beams.

The deck beams you're going to scribe with the jig fit under the sheer clamps, and in **Figure 21-2** the 5/8 x ¾-inch sheer clamps are in place. I like to

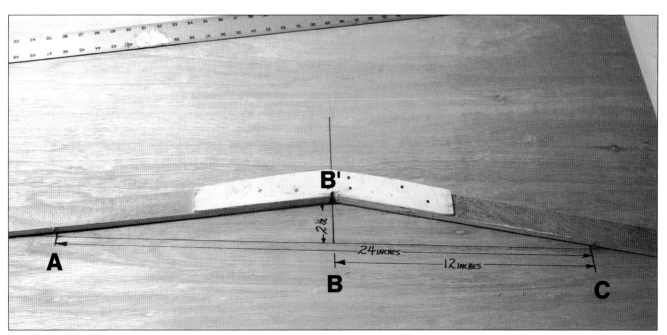

Figure 21-1

Figure 21-2

Figure 21-4

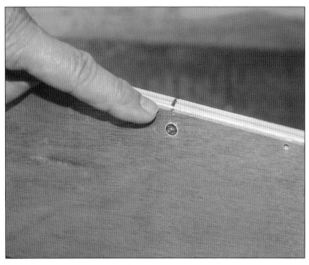

Figure 21-3

Figure 21-5

use spring clamps to hold the sheer clamp in place while I set the 6 x 5/8 screws. Be sure to countersink the screws, because the outwale goes over the top (**Figure 21-3**). When the dry fit is complete, epoxy both in place and set the screws (**Figure 21-4**). Of course do this at the other end of the boat as well.

The screws will allow you to continue to work even though the epoxy hasn't cured, but the clean-up will need to be thorough. In **Figure 21-5** the deck beams have been cut to length and are ready to install under the sheer clamp. The angle of the cut matches the angle of the hull and gives the maximum gluing surface under the sheer clamp (**Figure 21-6**). The close-up in **Figure 21-6** shows not only the angle of the cut but also how the beam upright has been trimmed back to allow the beam to fit under the sheer clamp. The deck beams are

Figure 21-6

Figure 21-7

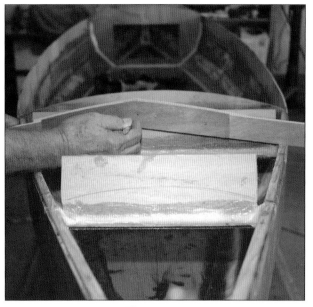

Figure 21-8

Figure 21-9

spaced 12 inches and 24 inches from the bulkhead.

In **Figure 21-7** a bead of epoxy has been applied to the upright section of the deck beam and to the area where the sheer clamp and deck beam join. Once these two beams are in place, move to the other end of the boat and do the same.

The epoxy will take awhile to cure, and it needs to be hard for the beams to marked and trimmed. When it has hardened, take the jig and use it much like a compass to scribe a line on the deck beam. A pencil fits in the apex of the two legs and marks the surface as the jig is moved from one side of the boat to the other (**Figure 21-8**). Now there is nothing left to do but plane down to the line. The Japanese keyhole saw will make quick work of the rough cut and shorten the amount of time planing (**Figure 21-9**).

With the deck beams cambered, it is getting easier to see what the finished boat will look like. It doesn't take much imagination to cover the decks and see the boat carrying you across a placid lake with only the sounds of your paddle in water and the magical cry of the loon in the distance.

22

False Stems

There are three main reasons to put a false stem on your boat. The false stem allows for a sharper entry in water for the bow and a smoother path as it flows past the stern. It also helps seal the planks against water entry where they join the stem. This is more important on boats with traditional construction, but stopping water entry is important even on a small glued lapstrake canoe. The last reason is the one we are most concerned with here: appearance. A false stem just adds a finished look to the boat. It makes the boat look more attractive. It does the other two jobs as well, but its main function on these boats is looks.

As with all jobs in boatbuilding, there's more than one way to fit false stems to the boat. Greg Rossel details a very nice way to laminate a stem and false stem in *WoodenBoat* issue 189, March-April 2006. This is certainly an excellent way to do the job, but it requires making the decision at the start of building the boat, because you make the stem and false stem at the same time.

I have built false stems by laminating them on the boat itself. It wasn't an easy task but very doable. I only did a few that way and then started to look for another method.

The method I use now is easy—I can fit a false stem in less time than it would take to set up the jigs of the other methods. That doesn't make this way better, it's just the one I use.

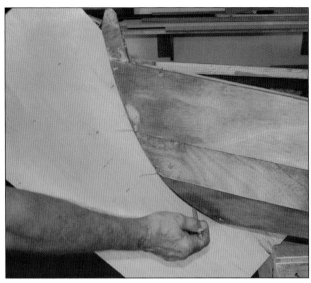

Figure 22-1

In **Figure 22-1** a scrap piece of plywood has been placed next to the bow and the shape of the bow traced. It will be important to have the boat firmly secured to keep it from shifting. Notice that tick marks have been put at upper chine and lower chine. These registration marks are important when doing the final fitting.

Cut the shape with a fine-tooth saber saw and put it up on the boat. Make notes with your pencil where the high spots are and use the wood rasp to take them down. When hand fitting, a small amount goes a long way, so be careful and remove very small amounts. Check the fit frequently and before you know it you'll have a very good fit (**Figure 22-2**).

This is your pattern that will transfer the shape of the stem to the wood used for the false stem. I used a 5-inch by 24-inch piece of 4/4 lyptus, a plantation-grown wood. 4/4 wood is the lumberyard designation for wood that is at least 1 inch thick rather than the thickness of a 1 x 4, which is ¾ inch thick. Remember that a 2x4 isn't 2 inches thick by 4 inches wide.

I like to use plantation-grown woods like lyptus and Spanish cedar because I think it's better environmental policy. I'm sure there are those who would disagree, but that's my personal belief. I've

Figure 22-2

Figure 22-4

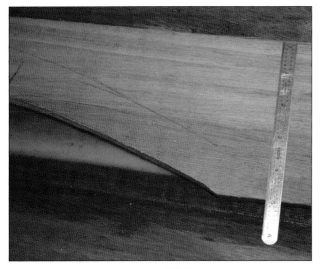

Figure 22-3

Figure 22-5

also used a short piece of 2 x 6 clear fir I picked up at the big building supply chains. All of the above will make attractive false stems.

Whatever wood you choose, transfer the shape to it and then draw another line 1½ inches over and roughly parallel to the first (**Figure 22-3**). Then cut out the shape of the stem—but don't cut out the other line yet. Leave that edge square for now. Put the piece up on the boat and do any fitting necessary (**Figure 22-4**).

When you have a good close fit, mark the centerline on the inside and drill a 3/16-inch hole

right on the centerline. Keep the drill as vertical as possible so the bit exits at centerline on the other side. In **Figure 22-5** a drill press was used, and a square block helped keep the false stem upright. However, this can be easily done with a hand drill. I've done it, but do use the square block to capture the false stem and keep it vertical. Just take your time and check to keep the drill perpendicular in both directions.

In **Figure 22-6** the false stem is back on the boat and the other line has been cut so the false stem now has its approximate final shape. A

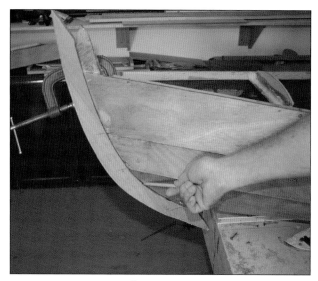

Figure 22-6

Figure 22-8

Figure 22-7

Figure 22-9

C clamp placed at the top will hold the false stem against the boat for a good look at the fit. You may need to take very small amounts off here and there, but this shouldn't be much of a task.

Also, a pencil line marks the thickness of the hull on the inside of the false stem. Later, you'll plane down to this line so the thickness of the false stem and hull is the same.

When you're satisfied with the fit and all the tweaking is done, drill a hole into the hull/stem using the 3/16 hole as a pilot (**Figure 22-7**). You will have to countersink this hole, and it will be best to use a taper drill bit with a countersink. I find a 10

x 2 or maybe a 10 x 2½ wood screw works best. You'll want about ¾- to 1-inch penetration into the stem so set the depth of the countersink accordingly.

In **Figure 22-8** the two screws have been set and the false stem is checked one last time for fit before it's shaped. The two screws are visible in **Figure 22-9** and should always be left standing proud—at least ½ inch clear of the inside of the false stem. These will guide the false stem and the screws back into the same place each time. Note that the approximate position of the screws is about an inch above the lower chine and an inch above the upper

Figure 22-10

chine. The screws have been backed, off and it's ready to be removed for shaping.

Figure 22-10 shows the false stem with one side being planed down. A centerline was drawn and then two lines each ¼ inch on either side were struck. A flexible ruler will make this job much easier. The two lines on either side of the centerline determine the amount of taper.

I like to start at the front and work toward the back. Planing down to the front line and then carrying the taper back works best for me. This helps prevent removing too much on the back side where you want the hull and false stem to be the same thickness. Don't hesitate to pop the false stem back up on the boat to check your progress. It's simple to take a little more off but very hard to put a little back on.

When you have the taper just right and the back edge of the false stem and the hull are a match, then set both stems aside until it's time to epoxy them on the boat.

Now there will be a few moments to rest and admire your craftsmanship. For me, the hand fitted stems provide a nice sense of accomplishment because they are cut from a solid piece of wood and made to fit on the boat. They are a point of pride for me and they should be for you as well.

23

Finishing Out the Hatches

There's one last job to do before you put on the decks and that's to finish out the hatches. You installed the basic framework when you cut out the bulkhead, but there's a bit more to do.

In order for the hatches to be anything approaching watertight, you will need to add a lip to the inside edge of the opening, set four threaded inserts, four 2½-inch ¼ x 20 stainless-steel machine screws, and add foam tape to the inside of the hatch cover.

You'll need the dimension from the back of the cleat to the face of the bulkhead to find the width of the lip (**Figure 23-1**). This dimension was 7/8 inch for Little Princess, and that made the overall width 1 5/8 inches in order to have the lip extend

Figure 23-1

beyond the face of the bulkhead ¾ inch (**Figure 23-2**). Notice that the vertical or short pieces fit inside the horizontal or long pieces. This makes assembly much easier because the short pieces support the longs. When you get a good dry fit, coat all the pieces and epoxy them in place with peanut butter epoxy using spring clamps as in **Figure 23-2**. It will be particularly important to clean up any squeeze-out on the face of the bulkhead and the lip. So wipe up all the epoxy with extra care.

Figure 23-2

While the epoxy is curing on hatches, you can make the covers. Carefully measure the outside dimensions of the hatch lip and add 1/8 inch to each measurement. Those dimensions were 15 inches x 7 ¼ inches for Little Princess and, with 1/8 added to each measurement, made the inside dimension for the hatch cover 15 1/8 x 7 3/8 inches.

In **Figure 23-3** the hatch cover was made using ¾ x ¾ cleat material epoxied to a 4mm piece of 1088 ply. The small nail holes show that it was tacked down while the epoxy cured. Also note that the inside was very thoroughly cleaned of all excess squeeze-out. Just as with the bulkhead and lip face, the epoxy must be wiped up for the hatch cover to fit.

I like to use 4mm that is about an inch larger than the OD of the cover and nail the cleats to it. Be sure

Figure 23-3

Figure 23-4

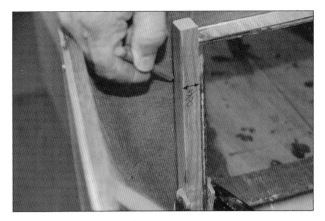

Figure 23-5

Figure 23-6

Figure 23-7

to make the frame square or it won't fit around the lip on the bulkhead. Once the epoxy has cured, I trim it down to the cleats. A router with a trim bit makes fast work of it, but trimming with a saw and then planing down to the cleat works equally well.

Now turn your attention back the hatches while the epoxy goes off on the covers. Carefully measure the width of the cleat on the back side of the bulkhead (**Figure 23-4**). For Little Princess this was 5/8 inch. You'll want to transfer that measurement to the face of the bulkhead by using a 5/8 piece of cleat material to strike a line (**Figure 23-5**) and then drilling a 3/8 inch hole on centerline (**Figure 23-6**). I like to drill 1 inch in from the top and bottom —this gives plenty of clearance for the knobs that hold the cover in place.

The holes are for the threaded inserts (**Figure 23-7**) that take the 2½-inch-long ¼ x 20 stainless-steel machine screws. The threaded inserts can be either

stainless steel or brass, but I prefer the stainless steel.

To install the inserts use a ¼ x 20 bolt with a hex head and 7/16-inch wrench. Two jam nuts on the bolt will make backing out the bolt from the insert much easier (**Figure 23-8**). Just put the insert on the bolt and push it into the hole while turning the bolt with the wrench. Run the insert all the way in the 3/8-inch pilot hole and then back off the jam nuts and remove the bolt, leaving the insert.

Next, run the 2½-inch bolts into the inserts so

Figure 23-8

Figure 23-10

Figure 23-9

Figure 23-11

they extend just ¼ inch beyond the face of the bulkhead and fit the hatch cover over the lip. Now just lightly tap the cove so the bolts will leave a mark on the inside of the cover. Remove the cover and drill a 5/16-inch hole at each mark. Be sure to label top and bottom on the inside of the cover because the cover will generally only fit one way.

Make sure the cover slides over the bolts easily; then you'll have to remove both of the lower corners to clear the fillet (**Figure 23-9**). Put some sealer behind each bolt to hold them in place and stop leaks, and run them completely tight against the insert (**Figure 23-10**). Also the foam tape has been added to the inside of the cover for a better

seal. Once all this is done, repeat at the other end of the boat.

I like to round the corners of the hatch cover for no other reason than it looks better than the square corners. In **Figure 23-11** the cover is ready to be coated and varnished. I varnish hatch covers and decks rather than painting them. The decks and covers can be varnished in a short amount of time, and it adds a huge amount to the appearance of the boat.

24

Epoxy the Decks

As the boat gets farther and farther along, the temptation will be to hurry, to finish so the boat can be on the water. This temptation will be particularly strong if the weather is getting warmer. But resist it and take your time putting on the decks and with the rest of the boat. I've found that I was always glad when the job was done right and always sorry when it wasn't.

The first step in putting on the decks will be to cut the stems flush with the sheer line (**Figure 24-1**). This will allow the 3mm plywood to lie flush so it can be temporarily nailed in place to be marked and cut.

Next, coat the interior of the boat with epoxy. Make sure that the sheer clamps get a good coat on the underside. This will keep them from absorbing any moisture and causing problems. I've seen clamps and cleats absorb enough moisture to swell and force deck seams open.

While the epoxy is curing on the interior, tack a 48-inch by 30-inch piece of 3mm plywood over the bulkhead and stem at one end of the boat (**Figure 24-2**) and trace around the hull (**Figure 24-3**).

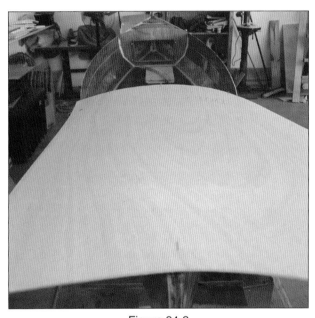
Figure 24-2

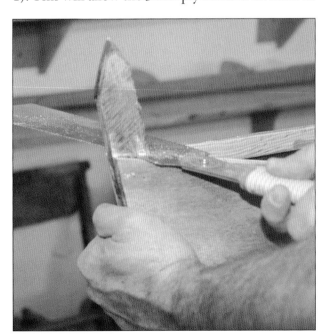
Figure 24-1

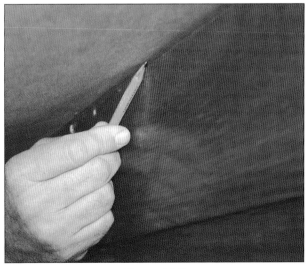
Figure 24-3

Figure 24-4

Figure 24-6

Figure 24-5

Figure 24-7

the sheer clamps with generous amounts of thickened epoxy. In **Figure 24-6** the sheer clamps have yet to be coated.

Now all that is left to do is temporarily nail the deck in place while the epoxy sets (**Figure 24-7**). It will be a good idea when the deck is nailed in place to reach in the compartment and, with a double-gloved hand, spread the epoxy out to create a small fillet on the deck beam (**Figure 24-8**). Note that the epoxy between the sheer clamp and the deck has also been spread into a small fillet, and that there is a generous layer of epoxy on top of the

With the piece on a flat surface, cut about ¾ inch outside the line (**Figure 24-4**) and coat the underside of the deck with epoxy using a disposable brush (**Figure 24-5**).

Leave the wet, rough-cut deck on the table and mix up some crunchy peanut butter epoxy. Because this is on the inside of the deck and won't be seen, you don't have to use wood flour to color the epoxy. You'll want to cover the top of the deck beams and

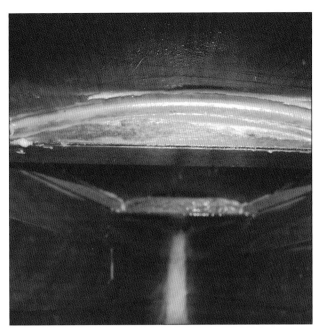

Figure 24-8

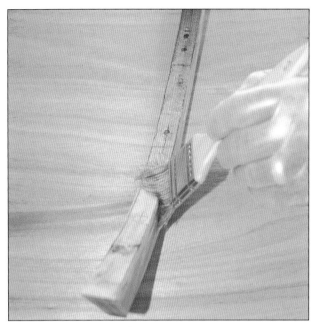

Figure 24-10

Figure 24-9

and evenly spaced, say 6 inches apart, as a design element of the boat. If it were done right, it could add a nice touch to the look of the boat. That being said, I have never experienced any failures with just the epoxy because I make sure to be generous spreading it and put the deck on when it is still wet.

After the epoxy has cured, trim the excess plywood with a saw and plane (**Figure 24-9**) and get ready to epoxy on the false stem.

It probably wouldn't be a bad idea to put the false stems up on the boat one last time to check the fit. I am a big believer in dry fitting because it can save so many headaches and panic situations with wet epoxy.

In **Figure 24-10** the false stem is coated with epoxy after it was taken down from the last dry fit. Remember, this keeps the joint from being glue starved. A close look shows where wood was removed right to where the lines were drawn on the back side.

sheer clamp. This is an area where you want the maximum amount, because the epoxy is all that is holding the deck to the sheer clamp.

In the past I have used boat nails driven into the sheer clamp as a mechanical fastener, but I never liked the way they looked and always covered them with a strip of trim. I've thought about, but never used, bronze or stainless-steel screws countersunk

Figure 24-11

Figure 24-12

Once everything is well coated, mix crunchy peanut butter epoxy, colored with wood flour, and put a thick layer over the inside (**Figure 24-11**). Note that the area around the screws has been left uncoated and that both screws stand proud, making it simple to find the exact screw holes in the hull/stem.

Figure 24-12 shows the squeeze-out as the screws are drawn tight, and **Figure 24-13** shows the false stem in place and all the excess epoxy removed. The last three steps have been followed to the letter. And of course the process is the same for the other end of the boat.

At this point, the launch party is getting closer with each completed task. But don't allow the anticipation of the launch to keep you from spending a few moments admiring the boat and maybe taking a short paddle up to the Territory Ahead.

Figure 24-13

25

Epoxy the Outwales and Inwales

Figure 25-1

Figure 25-2

Putting the outwales on the boat for the final time actually goes fairly quickly because you have already put them on once, when you set the sheer line. So this is just a matter of putting them back up and setting some screws.

Remember that in Chapter 19, **Figure 19-4**, that the outwale broke at a point where a screw had been set. Another outwale was put in place, and the sheer line was set and trimmed. When that outwale was put back up this time, it broke as well. Two more were tried, and they both broke at approximately the same spot. I came to the conclusion that either the piece of lyptus I was using as the outwale had a flaw in the plank or the plank was too brittle to take the curve. I had a choice of going back to the lumber yard and starting with a new piece of Lyptus or choosing another type of wood. I had a suitable piece of fir at hand, and that made it faster and more convenient to go with fir.

When I put the new piece of fir up on the boat, I discovered it was too proud (too stiff) to take the bend without changing the shape of the hull. To combat this I added a spacer/brace cut to the exact dimension of the inside hull, screwing it in place with temporary screws (**Figure 25-1**). This was

sufficient to allow the new fir outwale to take the bend without changing the shape of the hull, and work continued on as normal.

In **Figure 25-2** the outwale is clamped at the bow and stern as well as appropriate spots along the cockpit. Because the decks were now in place, no clamps were set in that area. Screws were set in the old holes (**Figure 25-3**) and the clamps in the cockpit removed.

Figure 25-4 shows where the false stem prevents the untrimmed outwale from lying flush against the hull. To trim the outwale, just measure the gap at the base of the false stem, in this case ¼ inch, and transfer that dimension to the end of the outwale, indicated by the pencil line and the X. This give the wedge shape that needs to be removed for

Figure 25-3

Figure 25-4

the outwale to lie flush. You'll need to do this at the stern as well.

I have always found it much easier to cut and trim the outwale in place rather than remove it from the boat. The Japanese saw will make very fast work of this cut; in **Figure 25-5** it's ready for the screw to be set.

I like to set screws on 12-inch intervals in the outwale. It won't work out exactly and you'll probably have to juggle a bit toward the bow and stern, but as long as the screws look evenly spaced it'll be fine.

Start at Station #5 and work your way toward either end of the boat (**Figure 25-6**). In **Figure 25-7** the spacing had to be compressed a bit toward the stern. It just takes a little trial and error to work out the spacing. Once the spacing is down, drill and countersink the hole (**Figure 28-8**). I countersink the holes because I use contrasting plugs as a design element. Also, I find 6 x ¾ stainless screws work well where the outwales screw into the sheer clamp under the deck.

When all the screws have been set, move to the other side of the boat and attach that outwale using the same process you just completed. In **Figure 25-9** the both outwales have been dry fitted and are ready to be epoxied to the boat.

This is done exactly the same way the planks were done. Unscrew everything just past #5 and coat the inside of the outwale with epoxy. It will be

Figure 25-5

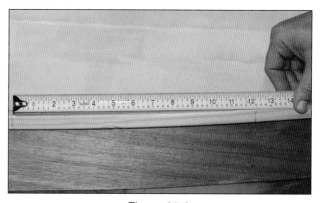

Figure 25-6

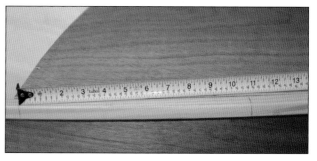

Figure 25-7

Figure 25-8

Figure 25-9

Figure 25-10

Figure 25-11

best to start at the bow and work your way aft to #5. Unlike the planks, there is a great deal of energy stored in that bent outwale, and it can give the unwary a nasty surprise or break.

When that section is coated, then butter the inside of the outwale with crunchy peanut butter epoxy. Be sure to add wood flour and try to match the color of the fir or the plywood. You don't want to pile too much epoxy on, but try to get an even layer.

As you work your way back to the bow, you may notice that areas stand out from the hull. In the cockpit a clamp will pull everything up tight, but the area around the deck presents another story. Here clamps want to slide off toward the bow or stern and will require a little help to stay in place. In **Figure 25-10** additional clamps have been added to keep the bar clamps from sliding off toward the stern. **Figure 25-11** shows a close-up of how a C clamp stops the bar clamp from slipping off.

Once all the clamps are set, you can turn your attention to the last three steps of clean up, clean up, and clean up.

The underside of the outwale needs to have absolutely all the squeeze-out wiped up. Trying to sand off hardened epoxy in this area will be very challenging.

I have found that it is best to epoxy one side, let that harden, and then do the other. Trying to jug-

Figure 25-12

gle two wet outwales before the epoxy goes off is too much. If you lose the race to have it all clamped and in place before the epoxy cures, you have cost yourself days undoing the mess. It's better to do one side then the other. It will take one day for each side or days and days if you gamble and lose.

While it's best to do only one outwale in a day, you can do both inwales in the same day. That's because it's fast and easy to clamp the inwale down in the cockpit area.

Figure 25-12 shows the interior of the boat primed, but the very top of the sheer plank was masked off to keep that area bare. Should you prime the interior before the inwales are set, it will be necessary to mask that area off. The primer will create a very weak bond, because the epoxy adheres to the primer and not the wood. I primed the interior thinking it would save some time but wound up having to work around the primer every time I wanted to epoxy something to the hull. I don't recall why I thought it would be a good idea and suggest that you wait until everything is down on the boat before you start to paint.

In **Figure 25-12** a single spring clamp holds the inwale with one end against the bulkhead; in **Figure 25-13** the angle of the bulkhead is transferred to the inwale. It will be simplest to make this cut off the boat (**Figure 25-14**) and then reclamp it on the boat. Try to clamp as close to the aft bulkhead as possible (if you started at the bow) and still have

Figure 25-13

Figure 25-14

Figure 25-15

Figure 25-16

Figure 25-18

Figure 25-17

the inwale sit on the deck while you transfer that angle (**Figure 25-15**). In this case, the cut is made on the boat with a Japanese saw (**Figure 25-16**) and then lowered into position. It might be better to cut it a hair longer and then make one final trim cut. When the fit is just right, then the same thing is done on the other side.

This method will give you a good fit, but there are certainly other ways to fit the inwales. Tom Hill

in his book *Ultralight Boatbuilding* details yet another way, and there are several "how to build" articles in *WoodenBoat* magazine that show some alternative methods.

Whatever method is used, the end result is both inwales clamped and epoxied in place (**Figure 25-17**). Once the clamps can come off, finish drilling and countersinking the remainder of the screw holes. You've already marked the outwale at 12-inch intervals; now mark the inwale so that screws fall between the screws on the outwale (**Figure 25-18**). I like to use 6 x 1-inch stainless for this, because that gives plenty of bury in the opposite wale.

When the screws are set, plug the holes with a contrasting-color plug dipped in varnish rather than epoxy. At one time I used epoxy but it was pointed out in an article I read that varnish would be much easier to deal with if the screws ever needed to come out. So use varnish and when it dries, trim the plugs flush with a chisel or a flush-cut trim saw.

You can also just set the screws slightly below the surface and then sand flush to them instead of using countersunk plugs. It looks good but the screws always fill with varnish, and that detracts from the overall appearance.

With the plugs cut flush, the boat looks very good sitting on the sawhorses or strongback. At this point with virtually every boat I have built and probably will build, I start to get impatient. It seems that there is very little left to do—and in one sense that's true. However, there are a number of small jobs that add up to a fair amount of time.

I have had impatience turn to gloom as it seems like the boat will never be finished. In one dark moment, I felt very much like Sisyphus. He rolled the stone up the mountain only to have to do again, and it seemed that for every job I did, there was one just like it taking its place.

Well, that's a small exaggeration, but it does seem sometimes like the boat will take forever to finish. However, I have learned that this is a fleeting moment, and I no longer give in to gloomy thoughts. Continue looking at each small task as a whole, as a unit by itself, rather than one small piece of a puzzle. That will give you immediate gratification and make it easier to keep checking off the jobs because the boat is very close to being finished.

26

Finishing Out the Boat

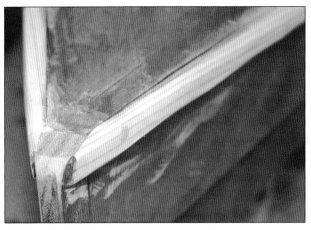

Figure 26-2

There are several small jobs left to do for the boat to be finished out. Most of them will go quickly—and that is, of course, a good thing. Doing the jobs in a particular order will also help speed the process along and give a better sense of progress.

The first place to start is on the outwales. With the plugs cut flush with a chisel or flush-cut trim saw, the next step is to taper the outwales at the bow and stern. I like to start back about 10 or 12 inches with a block plane and slowly remove wood until the end is planed down to about 1/16, maybe an 1/8 inch. **Figure 26-1** shows the contrast of the tapered and untapered side. Once both sides are

tapered, it will be a good time to take the block plane and round over the entire length of the out-wale. How much to round it is a matter of personal taste, but I take about 1/8 inch off the top and bottom edge. Use the plane to round over any crisp or sharp edges, and finish off with the sander.

In **Figure 26-2** both sides have been tapered and the false stem has been trimmed flush with the deck. Round and shape the false stem to remove sharp edges and corners. A wood rasp and sander will do this job quickly and nicely.

When the top is completed, turn your attention to the false stem on the bottom. Flip the boat over and trim off the extra. The Japanese saw works very well for this, because it can be held flat against the

Figure 26-1

Figure 26-3

bottom as a guide while the cut is made (**Figure 26-3**). Round over all sharp corners and sand the front edge to remove any lines and soften all the curves. Eighty-grit sandpaper removes wood very fast and should be followed by 150 grit over the false stems and the entire length of the outwales.

In **Figure 26-4** a 3/8-inch hole has been drilled in the false stem at the bow and the stern. This will allow a 3/8-inch-rope carrying strap to be secured to the false stem. A countersink will ease the edges of the hole and help eliminate abrasion of the rope (**Figure 26-5**). **Figure 26-6** shows the carrying strap in place and ready to use.

With the taper cut, the outwales sanded, and the false stems finished, you can now move to the interior of the boat. There are really only three jobs to be done in the interior, and they are all very straightforward. Probably the easiest are the eight ¾ x ¾ x 2-inch blocks epoxied to the bottom. Start with ¾-inch square stock, cut eight 2-inch pieces, and then round the corners. Coat them, put peanut butter epoxy on the bottom and set them in the approximate location shown in **Figure 26-7**. **Figure 26-8** is a close-up of a block and the pad eye that will be screwed to each block. The 2-inch length cramps the pad eye some; a 2½-inch length

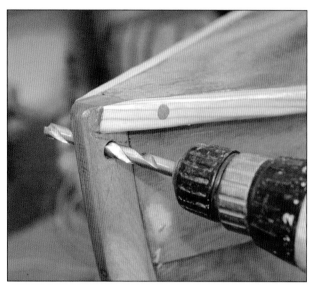

Figure 26-4

Figure 26-6

Figure 26-5

Figure 26-7

would be better (note that the primer has been removed under the blocks so the epoxy will get a good bond).

These blocks and pad eyes provide tie-downs for any cargo and an anchor for the kayak seat (**Figure 26-9A**). I use a store-bought box to carry loose gear and provide a raised seat (**Figure 26-9B**). Criss-crossed bungee cords attached to the pad eyes capture the box firmly in place. For a short paddle the box would be overkill, but the area will also hold a small ice chest, and a cold drink on a hot day is most welcome.

The next job, putting a face plate on the bulk-head, is a little more involved, but still an easy task. I've used a 1/8-inch-thick by 2½-inch-wide by 30-inch-long piece of lyptus that I cut on the table saw. Cutting a tall, thin piece on a table saw can be challenging, so be very careful and use push sticks.

If you don't have a table saw, a piece of 4mm plywood or 6mm plywood would work too. If you use the plywood, be sure to use at least three coats of epoxy on the end grain/edge after you trim it to shape.

The lyptus was cut to the length indicated by the arrows in **Figure 26-10** and, using a block to raise the pencil to 5/16 inch, a line was struck that

Figure 26-8

Figure 26-9B

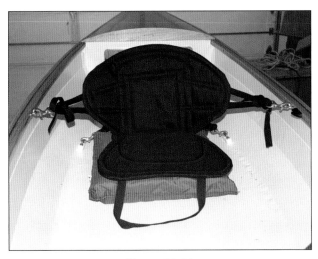

Figure 26-9A

Figure 26-10

Figure 26-11

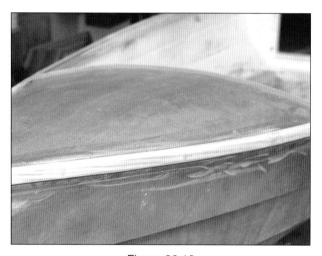

Figure 26-12

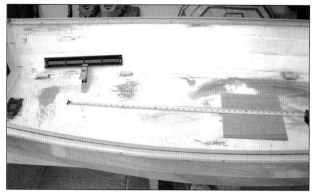

Figure 26-13

Figure 26-14

followed the deck's camber (**Figure 26-11**). Then the face plate was pulled off the boat and trimmed to the line. It might be better to just use a plane on the lyptus or other solid wood, because a saber saw can split out your piece. Once trimmed and sanded, it was first coated and then epoxied in place with peanut butter epoxy colored with wood flour (**Figure 26-12**). The last three steps were religiously followed with any squeeze-out.

The last addition to the interior is a footrest. A footrest is important to any boat paddled like a kayak, sitting on the bottom of the boat and using a double-bladed paddle. It allows you to brace your feet for a more efficient paddle stroke and general comfort.

In **Figure 26-13** the plywood square is placed just aft of Station #5 and represents the location of the seat. The tape measure is placed so 33 inches is centered on the square. The adjustable footrest is positioned so its center is either on or just aft of the end of the tape. This will be about right for individuals 6 feet tall and slightly under. Those taller than 6 feet will need to adjust the footrest accordingly. The best way to accomplish this is with the boat on flat ground and the person seated in the boat. With your knees slightly bent to a comfortable position, place a pencil mark on the side of the boat and place the footrest to match the mark (**Figure 26-14**). The adjustable brace allows the canoe to be trimmed as cargo and weight are added. Those not wanting to use the adjustable brace (see the appendix for the supplier) can use a fixed footrest like the design in **Figure 26-15**.

With the footrest epoxied in place, the last task before painting is to give the entire boat at least one coat of epoxy. Those areas to be varnished should get at least two coats and a sanding with 150-grit

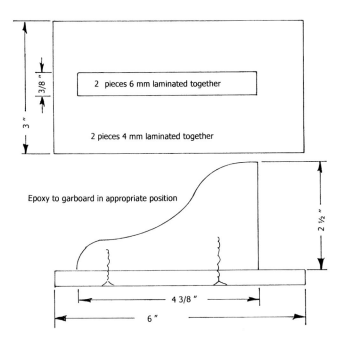

2 pieces 6 mm laminated together

2 pieces 4 mm laminated together

3/8"

3"

Epoxy to garboard in appropriate position

2 1/2"

4 3/8"

6"

Figure 26-15

Figure 26-16

sandpaper in between coats. Use a disposable brush (a 3-inch-wide one works very well) and get as smooth a surface as possible (no runs or drips). This will mean less sanding before painting and varnishing (**Figure 26-16**).

There are two things to remember about coating the boat with epoxy: Do it toward the end of the day as it starts to get cooler, and don't do it in direct sunlight. This will be more important if the tem-

peratures are higher, like in the summer.

The wood has air in its pores, and the epoxy traps that air in the pores. As the temperature rises, that air expands and creates tiny, or sometimes not-so-tiny, bubbles in the epoxy. Those bubbles are caused by what is called outgassing. This is something you want to avoid, so remember: Shade moves, and in warm weather start in the cooler part of the day. I didn't . . . one time.

When the epoxy has cured, sand the boat with 150-grit sandpaper. Pay particular attention to any runs or drips, as these will show through the paint. The goal is to get as smooth a surface as possible, because it's the quality of the base that will mostly determine the quality of the final coat of paint.

In chapter 1 I cautioned you against lavishing hours of time on painting the boat—I felt this was just wasting time that could be spent using the boat. So let me temper the last paragraph with a small caveat. Don't worry about minor flaws; focus on the major drips and big runs of epoxy. The minor stuff will not be noticed after you have had the boat in the water. What constitutes a major or minor flaw? Well, you will have to determine that because after all it is your boat, but don't spend hours going after little flaws in out-of-the-way places.

So with that small caveat out of the way, let's move on to the paints. I used Interlux Brightside paints and primers for years, and these are excellent products. There are others that are just as good, but Brightside served me well. It stands up well and is fairly hard so it doesn't scratch easily; when it does, the surface is simple to touch up.

I used Interlux for years, but now I've switched to a water-based polyurethane paint by System Three. I changed for two reasons: It's healthier for me and the planet, and it's a good product that cleans up with water.

Whatever paint you choose, always follow the directions to the letter. Apply the paint within the recommended temperature range and be very care-

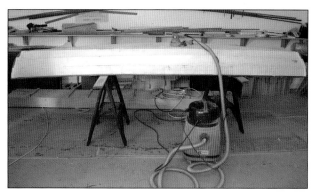

Figure 26-17

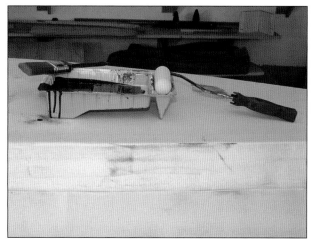

Figure 26-18

ful with flammable products . . . Now let's paint.

In **Figure 26-17** the boat has the outwales and false stems masked off, a coat of primer has been applied, and it has been sanded with 220-grit paper. The hull has been wiped down with the appropriate solvent—or water, in the case of System Three—and then wiped with a tack cloth. Basically the boat is ready for the first coat of paint.

I use a method of painting called rolling and tipping. It's simple and it's easy to get good results. In the past I have sprayed boats with HVLP guns and regular spray guns, but I have stopped. The equipment is expensive, it's hard to master the technique, and it's not very healthy.

There are a number of shops that paint boats, large and small, by rolling and tipping, so there is no reason you can't get a professional finish doing exactly the same.

Figure 26-18 shows the "extensive" number of tools you'll need to paint your boat using rolling and tipping. The roller is foam; don't use a roller with nap, because the nap comes off in the paint. Forget what the package said and what the guy in the store told you . . . it will come off in the paint. The paintbrush is very inexpensive—just above disposable grade. And the roller tray is small and disposable as well. That's it. That's all you need to start rolling and tipping your boat.

You should start on the bottom. Roll out an area about 12 to 18 inches long and then drag the dry brush lightly over the paint. Always drag back toward the area just rolled out. Don't worry if it doesn't look very good. You're just learning, and it's on the bottom anyway. Continue to work your way across the bottom doing small sections at one time. The warmer the weather, the faster you'll have to work, and the smaller a section you'll paint.

When the bottom is done, move to the garboards. Do one garboard and then the other. Then move to the mid-plank and then the sheer. Try to catch any runs and sags with the brush as you go along. By the time you get to the last sheer plank, you will be fairly good.

In **Figure 26-19** the boat has the first coat of paint. Let the paint dry, the recommended time and then sand with 220 grit. Any sags or runs need to be sanded down at this point. If you go into the primer, spot the area with some paint and a disposable brush, let dry and lightly sand. This will help keep that area from showing through the second coat.

The second coat goes on just like the first, but now you'll be better at the technique. In **Figure 26-20** the stipple from the roller is visible; **Figure 26-21** shows the dry brush dragging over the roll-out.

Just continue in the same order as before and in no time the boat will be completely painted (**Figure 26-22**). As the paint dries, the brush marks will level out and disappear and leave a smooth, even

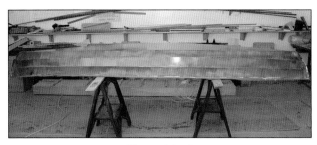

Figure 26-19

Figure 26-20

Figure 26-21

Figure 26-22

surface. A paint job you can be proud of . . .

When the paint has dried, remove the masking tape, turn the boat over, and paint the interior. The interior will be slightly different, because there are areas that can't be rolled—they are too small, or there are blocks in the way. So I roll the bottom but don't tip (I like at bit of stipple on the bottom for traction), and brush out the rest of the interior. Watch for runs and sags and try to catch them with the brush. The first coat should cover the primer if the interior color is light, which it should be. I find that an off white is much gentler on the eyes than a hard white.

With the interior done, that leaves the wales and decks to be varnished. The varnish provides much needed protection for the epoxy from UV light. I have used Interlux Schooner varnish for a good many years and haven't found any I like better. It has a nice golden color that adds a warm honey tone to the decks and wales. I'm sure there are many varnishes that are as good; each shop seems to have its favorite. So you can't go wrong with any of the major brands.

Regardless of the brand, varnish work is preparation, preparation and preparation. Any of the many volumes—and there are many—make this very clear. If you decide to take varnishing to the next level, sit down and read several books on the subject.

If not, what you'll find here will serve you well. At this point, you should have at least two coats of epoxy on the decks and wales and it should have been sanded with 220 grit paper. If in sanding it smooth you broke through the epoxy into the wood, those areas should be touched up with epoxy and sanded. Once you have a good, sanded coat of epoxy, wipe it down with the appropriate solvent, followed by a tack cloth when the solvent dries.

Then find a cool place in the shade, or better yet inside. Wind, dust, leaves, and bugs are your enemies when varnishing, so look for an area as free from the above as possible. If it's cold, like the fall or winter, the space will need to be at least 50 degrees Fahrenheit. I won't start to varnish in my shop unless it's 60 degrees even though most brands say 50 degrees.

When I do start, I use the same type of brush I use to tip off the paint. You can spend more on a brush, and I have, but honestly I can't see the difference. Also, the solvent to clean the brushes is not cheap, and it takes a lot to get an expensive brush really clean. Now I use the cheaper brushes. In the past I used disposable brushes but I got tired of picking the little bristles out of the varnish.

So take the cheaper brush and apply a thin coat of varnish to the wales and decks. The most common mistake made is to apply too much varnish. Once the boat is coated, put the brush down and walk away. If you don't walk away then throw the brush in the garbage so it can't be used.

Here's what will happen with the brush in your hand: As you walk around the boat admiring the job—and it will look very nice—a holiday, a missed spot, will be noticed and you will succumb to the temptation to touch it up. That will just make a mess every time. How do I know that? I'd be embarrassed to tell you how many times I did it until I learned to walk away.

When you get to walk back depends on the drying time. If the drying time is, say, 16 hours, then wait 8 more before you sand with 220-grit paper. You want to allow plenty of time between coats, but this won't be easy because the boat looks great and is basically ready for the water. When I have rushed the next coat I have always been sorry. It usually results in a delay.

I like to put a minimum of three coats on and will do four or five if time permits. This just makes revarnishing faster when it needs to be done. In **Figure 26-23** the boat has two coats of varnish and is waiting for sanding and the next coat.

This is one of my favorite times because the boat looks beautiful, I can smell just a hint of varnish, and I start to think about all the places I plan to take the boat.

Figure 26-23

27

When Things Go Wrong

When I first started reading boatbuilding books, it seemed like every book talked about a crying chair or moaning chair. A chair where the shop owner would, at various times, sit and moan about his fate as a boatbuilder. This was, I suspect, just a metaphor for those times when something goes wrong—but then maybe not.

There may not be an actual crying chair, but things do go wrong every now and then. On the first boat I built, I had a sheer plank scarf let go. It was winter and I wanted the epoxy in the lap to cure faster than it was, so I moved a heater up close to the boat to expedite the curing. The general idea was if a little heat is good, a lot is better. I didn't realize that heat would soften and weaken epoxy until I heard the scarf give way. From that point on, I knew.

I stood there in looking at the failed scarf utterly dejected. All the work getting the boat this far was for nothing, I knew I was going to have to cut the boat up and start over. With my tail between my legs, I drove to get a cup of coffee and tried to figure out just how small those pieces needed to be. I was sitting in the crying chair whether I knew it or not.

Somewhere along the way for coffee it occurred to me that I could reglue the scarf—all was not lost.

Of course, all is never lost, and it was a simple fix. Most problems that occur are simple to fix once the solution is found.

I like to tell my students that there isn't a mistake that can't be fixed. Even cutting the boat in half can be fixed, so if something goes wrong just step back and find the solution. It's there, I promise.

Figure 27-1

A case in point is **Figure 27-1**. When I was gluing up the mid-plank on Little Princess I failed to give everything one last check before I walked away. Had I looked, the problem would have been caught and fixed then, but I didn't notice that the plank had sprung out and created a gap until after the epoxy had set. What caused the problem is immaterial, but I suspect that when I was setting the other plank the boat was pushed or twisted enough to cause the gap. The more important question was how to fix it.

I pulled out all the temporary nails and then, with the Japanese saw, cut away as much of the hardened epoxy as I could (**Figure 27-2**). With a baggie filled with peanut butter epoxy, I injected epoxy into the gap. A series of drywall screws pulled the plank up tight against the garboard.

Figure 27-2

I made sure the plank was fair and wiped up the squeeze-out (**Figure 27-3**).

It wasn't difficult and only took a little over an hour to do. I've used this solution to fix a stem that was off center. I've seen heat used to remove an entire plank from the boat. Remembering that heat softens epoxy can be very useful.

So the lesson here is: Sometimes mistakes happen, but it's not a disaster. Mistakes can be fixed. Don't worry and just build the boat.

Figure 27-3

28

Changing
the Plans

The cockpit in Little Princess is 6 feet long, so an individual 6 feet tall or less could lie down and sleep in the cockpit. But what if you're 6 feet 4 inches tall? What do you do then? Well, you move the bulkheads back a few inches to make the cockpit larger. It's not very involved to move the bulkheads, but you do need to make the decision before you start construction.

It's not difficult; in fact, you do everything exactly the same, but just leave the bulkheads off Stations #2 and #7. Every other step is identical until you turn the boat over.

With the boat turned over the interior is a blank slate, so to speak, and the bulkheads can be placed where you want them.

Once you decide the location of each bulkhead, the next step is to make a template. Find a piece of scrap plywood, mark it with a centerline, and tack on a cross brace at the height of the sheer. The template should be about 2 inches less than the width of the bottom. If the bottom is 15 inches wide where you want the bulkhead, then the template should be about 13 inches wide. Now secure the template in the boat so the centerline of the template and the centerline of the boat match. Make sure the template is perpendicular to the bottom and is in the location you want the bulkhead. It

won't be a bad idea to brace the bottom of the template as well, to keep it from moving.

When everything is locked in place, take a tick stick—a straight stick about 3 inches less than the width of the bottom—and place it so the corner sits right on the chine between the bottom and garboard. Now trace around the stick with a clear line and repeat the process for each chine on both sides of the boat (**Figure 28-1**).

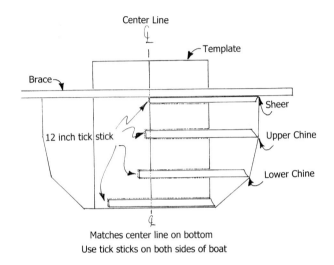

Figure 28-1

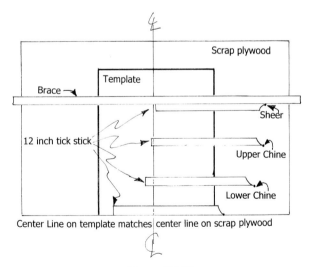

Figure 28-2A

At this point you could go straight to marine plywood and cut the bulkhead, but I've found it better to make one trial bulkhead first and cut the marine plywood from the trial bulkhead.

Cut away on both sides of the boat

Figure 28-2B

Figure 28-3

So take a piece of cheap ply that will be large enough and mark it with a centerline. Match the centerline of the template up with the centerline of cheap ply and transfer the chine points (**Figure 28-2A**). Connect the dots and cut out the trial bulkhead (**Figure 28-2B**). Check the fit, make any minor adjustments, and then trace that shape on the marine plywood. Be sure to transfer the centerline of the trial bulkhead to the marine plywood.

Before you cut it to shape, it will be best to lay out the hatch on the face and put the cleats in place. When everything is complete, then make the cut and tab it in place with epoxy. Once the epoxy has hardened, then come back and put in the fillets.

If you wanted to add a deck and combing like the boat in **Figure 28-3** then knees and supports can be fashioned using this process. **Figure 28-4** shows the framework that goes under the combings.

Moving a bulkhead or adding a coaming can take a good boat and tailor-fit it to your specific needs, making it even better. However, building the boat to the plans is faster and simpler than making changes. And moving away from the plans is always a compromise that may not be worth the effort, so some thought should precede making a change.

Should you decide it's worth the effort, now you have the knowledge to do the job.

Figure 28-4

29

Making Some Accessories

The Downwind Sail

Many of the decked double-paddle canoes that were built during the late 1800s and early 1900s carried a downwind sail. One of the most famous, John MacGregor's Rob Roy, made some very impressive voyages aided by a downwind sail, so it seemed natural that Little Princess and the other two canoes should have one as well.

I settled on using a sliding gunter sail. In the 1890s this was a popular sail for these canoes because it can set a large sail on a short mast and spar. There are other types of sails that could have been used, but I like the sliding gunter for its simplicity.

Figure 29-1 shows a sliding gunter with both mast and spar at 38 inches; this allows the mast and spar to fit in the forward compartment of all the canoes in this book. The luff is 44 inches and the foot is 40 inches, which gives a sail of about 6 square feet. Not much when you consider that some of those canoes set sails of 40 and 50 square feet. But all that square footage of sail came with an enormous amount of rigging and gear, which is far from simple.

While 6 square feet of sail may not compete with 40 or 50 square feet, it will provide a pleasant, relaxing run downwind and be easily managed by the most novice of sailors and canoeists. Also, with the mainsheet always held in a hand so it can be instantly released, the 6-square-foot sail presents little danger of causing a capsize.

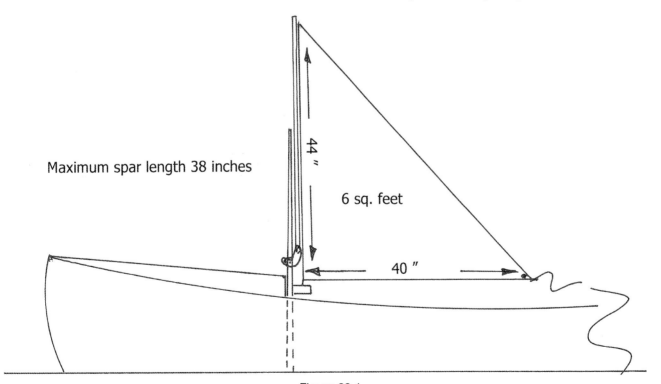

Maximum spar length 38 inches

44 "

6 sq. feet

40 "

Figure 29-1

But even the simple sail shown in **Figure 29-1** has several pieces, and some may find that the benefits don't outweigh the complications. Personally I feel the benefits are worth any small complications as well as the time and labor spent making the parts.

So if you decide to add a downwind sail, the decision will need to be made **before** the decks are put on, because a piece of backing needs to be added behind the bulkhead (**Figure 29-2**). This backing, a piece of ¾-inch-thick white pine, adds stiffness and gives the #10 x 2-inch-long stainless steel screws for the mast partner something to bite into. Once it's epoxied in place, the decks can be added and construction can proceed in the normal manner.

Figure 29-2

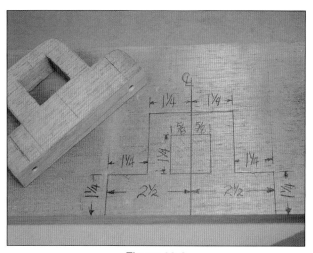

Figure 29-3

As you continue on with the construction, there will be downtime while you wait for epoxy to cure or just odd moments when you'll want to work on the boat but don't have a big block of time. You can use these moments to build all the parts that make up the downwind sail.

The first step will be to make the mast partner. **Figure 29-3** gives the dimensions of the mast partner that has been drawn on a piece of 1-inch-thick Spanish cedar. If Spanish cedar or another type of 1-inch-thick wood isn't available then laminate four pieces of 6mm scrap plywood; this will provide an attractive 1-inch-thick piece of material for the mast partner.

Once you have the material, lay out the dimensions with a square and cut it out. It will be a good idea to round the corners like the partner in **Figure 29-3**—sharp corners have no place on a boat. Then coat the partner with epoxy and set it aside in safe place.

Next, laminate two ¾ x 1½ x 42-inch-long pieces of clear (no knots) fir together to form a 1½ x 1½ square. When the epoxy has cured, rip that into a 1¼ x 1¼ square. This is the finished dimension of the mast and matches the 1¼ x 1¼ hole in the mast partner.

You'll cut a taper on the mast later but for now set the square mast aside and make the 1 x 1 x 40-inch-long square for the spar by laminating two pieces of fir together. Do this just like you made the mast and rip the square down to 1 inch by 1 inch. Set this square aside with the square for the mast and turn your attention to making the mast step.

Actually, the mast step is quite simple to make. I made the step for Little Princess from a 2½ x 4 piece of 3mm plywood with 3mm x 5/8-inch strips epoxied on to create a 1¼ x 1¼ inch square for the base of the mast (**Figure 29-4**).

Anything that would create the 1¼-inch square would work, but the hatch must be able to clear

Figure 29-4

Figure 29-5

Figure 29-6

the mast step. **Figure 29-4** shows about ½ inch of clearance between the top of the mast step and the bottom of the hatch.

With all the parts assembled, continue normal construction until the boat is ready to paint. When that point is reached, screw the mast partner to the bulkhead so the centerline of the partner matches the centerline of the boat. The top of the partner should be 11 inches from the bottom of the boat as well as level with it.

Now drop the mast square into the partner and place it on the mast step. Make sure the mast is perpendicular to the bottom, and that the bottom is level as well. This is best accomplished with two levels (**Figure 29-5**). When you have the mast perpendicular to the bottom clearly mark the location of the mast step and epoxy it in place with peanut-butter-thick epoxy.

At this point you can cut the taper on the mast and spar. The first step for cutting the taper is to strike a centerline on all four sides of the mast. Put the mast back in the partner and step and place a mark about 1 inch up from the top of the partner (**Figure 29-6**). If the epoxy hasn't cured on the mast step, be careful to not disturb its location as you remove it. Now moving to the other end or top of

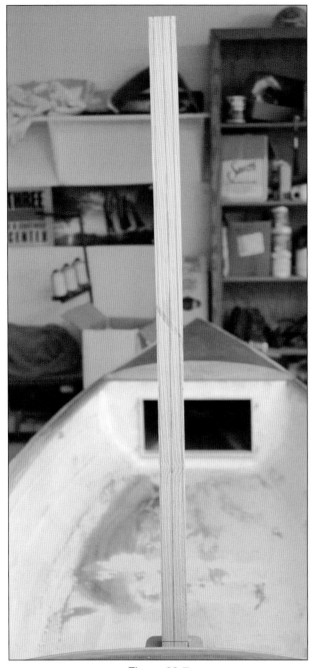

Figure 29-7

Figure 29-8

the mast, put a mark 3/8 inch on either side of the centerline on all four sides as well. This gives you the taper on the mast, and **Figure 29-7** shows the mast with the taper marked and ready to cut.

I have found that the easiest way to cut the taper is with a plane. I start with an 8-inch jack plane and then finish with a block plane for the fine work.

This is a very fast method and took me less than 30 minutes for the mast. I suspect that was less time than it would have taken to set up a taper jig, make the test cuts to get the adjustment just right, and then make all the cuts. I found using a plane not only faster but far more satisfying than pushing the wood through the table saw or cutting it on the band saw.

A word of caution is in order, however: It is amazing how fast a jack plane can remove wood. Unless care is taken, too much material can be taken off and the blank ruined. I was forced to rip a second blank for the mast because of lack of vigilance.

Figure 29-8 shows the second mast with the taper cut and a 5/16 hole drilled in the top for the halyard. Also, you'll want to relieve the hole so the halyard can run free with little or no chafe (**Figure 29-9**). With the hole for the halyard relieved, just coat the mast and set aside with the partner.

Figure 29-9

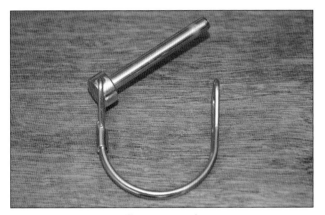

Figure 29-10A

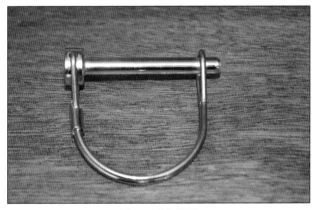

Figure 29-10B

Figure 29-11A

Now turn your attention to making the spar. Take the piece of laminated fir 1 inch by 1 inch by 40 inches long and cut the taper exactly the same way as you did with the mast. The spar tapers from 1 inch at the bottom to 5/8 inch at the top. Once the taper is cut, drill a 5/16 hole 15 inches up from the bottom of the spar and coat the spar with epoxy. The hole should be on centerline and is for the halyard.

Once the yard is planed down and squared up you'll want to turn your attention to rigging the halyard and finding a jaw for the base of the yard. When I was putting together the rigging for the sail, I didn't have any trouble finding the ¼-inch three-strand rope for the halyard, the two blocks, and a jam cleat, but the jaw for the gunter yard was quite another story. On other sliding gunters, a toggle or plywood jaws with parrel beads had worked just fine, but the small size of the mast made these solutions impractical or at least not the best. A steel ring with a diameter of 2 inches seized to the heel of the yard seemed like a good answer, but during the search for the ring a better solution was found. I stumbled on something called a coupler safety pin (see **Figures 29-10A** and **10B**).

The pin combined with a pad eye worked perfectly. Everything was easy to assemble or disassemble, and a pad eye kept the pin from sliding too far down the mast and jamming (**Figures 29-11A** and **29-11B**). You'll find the placement of the pad eye is important, and the two screw holes in **Figure 29-11B** show that the first try stopped the yard short of a full hoist. I suggest hoisting the yard with the pin in place and then marking the location of the pad eye (note that the pad eye is on the bow side of the mast), which is what I should have done the first time.

Now there was nothing left to do but place the two blocks and the jam cleat so the halyard follows

Figure 29-11B

the inwale on the port side (**Figure 29-12**) and do a test hoist to be sure it all functioned as intended (**Figures 29-13A, B,** and **C**).

In the original drawing I used to design the sail (**Figure 29-1**) I calculated a luff of 44 inches and a foot of 40 inches, but once the rig was tested I found I could achieve a luff of 50 inches. The extra 6 inches came from the gunter yard being able to carry a bit farther up the mast. I made a mock sail out of paper to check how everything would work —this will be a good idea for you to do as well (**Figure 29-14**).

Once you have the final measurements of the sail, make a drawing like the one I used in **Figure 29-15** and send it to your sailmaker. I did find that the hollow in the leech and the roach at the foot were not really necessary and could be dropped, particularly if it would add to the cost.

I ordered my sail from Duckworks (see the Suppliers appendix) and found it to be well made and a very good value. Chuck Leinweber and his sailmaker are knowledgeable people, and they go out of their way to get it right. Just remember that the

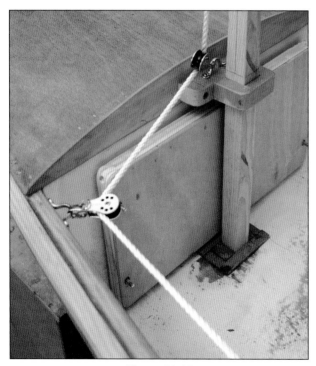

Figure 29-12

Figure 29-13A

Figure 29-13B

Figure 29-13C

Figure 29-14

the spar like **Figure 29-16A, B, C** and attach the tack of the sail like **Figure 29-17**. Let me repeat the caveat about keeping the mainsheet in your hand and not cleating it off. To do otherwise is inviting a capsize even with this small a sail. In **Figure 29-18** the mainsheet is held so it can be allowed to weathervane if a hard puff catches the sail abeam.

In my opinion a downwind sail is a perfect addition to these fine canoes and carries on the voyaging tradition from the 1880s.

sailmaker can't read your mind; make sure the drawing you send is exactly what you want.

While you are waiting on the sail to arrive, continue to paint the boat and add several coats of varnish to both the mast and spar.

When the sail arrives, bend (attach) the sail on

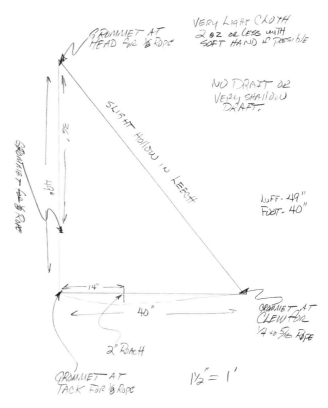

Figure 29-15

Figure 29-16A

Figure 29-16C

Figure 29-17

Figure 29-16B

Figure 29-18

Making a Double-Bladed Paddle

There are a large number of double paddles on the market, and all of them will do the job of moving your canoe through the water. The problem is that almost all of the paddles are designed for kayaks and not canoes. Because kayaks are narrower than canoes, the paddles are shorter, and longer paddles work best for a canoe like yours.

Most of the paddles in stores seem to be in the 220cm to 230cm range (paddle length is almost always given in centimeters), or about 87 to 91 inches. These paddles will work, but I have found double paddles around 235cm to 245cm (93 to 96 inches) work better.

The paddle length I find works the best is about 260cm, or 102 inches. Where did I buy a paddle this length? I didn't buy it. I made it, and you can too. All you need is an 8-foot section of 1 3/16 closet rod available at any chain building supply store, some scrap 6mm plywood, and a stainless-steel ferrule from Duckworks, if you want the paddle to break down.

Start by cutting the 8-foot closet rod into two four foot sections. Don't worry about being exact with your cut, because you'll trim some off before the ferrule goes on the paddle shaft.

In **Figure 29-19** half the rod has been cut away approximately 9 inches from the end and a mark has been made about 20 inches from the end. I made the initial cut that split the end of the rod in half on the table saw and then used a Japanese saw to square and clean up the cut.

Next, I clamped the rod to the worktable and cut a taper from the 20-inch mark to the end with a block plane. I found it easiest to first plane the end down to 5/8 inch and then work the taper back to the 20-inch mark. Exercise care and check your progress because it's easy to remove too much and have to start over. **Figure 29-20** shows the approx-

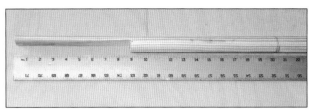

Figure 29-19

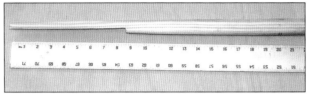

Figure 29-20

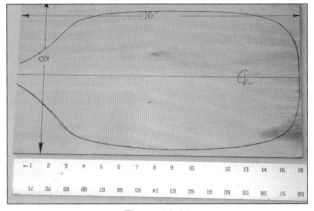

Figure 29-21

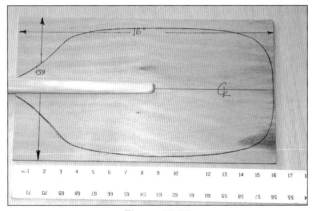

Figure 29-22

imate taper for the rod. When you have the taper on the first section, do exactly the same with second section of rod and set the two pieces aside.

Then take two 9-inch by 16-inch squares of 6mm plywood drop and mark a centerline on both sides. **Figure 29-21** shows a pattern for a blade drawn on the square as well. In **Figure 29-22** the rod is centered on the 6mm and checked for fit, then cut out (**Figure 29-23**).

I like to temporarily tack the 6mm ply to the rod with two finish nails, make sure everything is on centerline, then set three #6 x 5/8 stainless steel screws (**Figure 29-24**).

Now epoxy the 6mm to the rod using peanut-

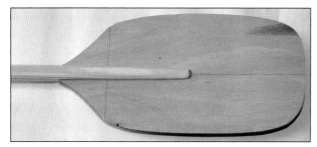

Figure 29-23

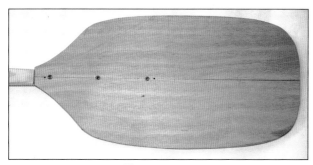

Figure 29-24

Figure 29-25

Figure 29-26

butter-thick epoxy. The #6 screws will act as registration pins, so don't cover the screw holes with epoxy (**Figure 29-25**). Take the squeeze out and create small fillets where the rod meets the blade. If you wait until the fillet is almost set—firm but still pliable—brushing the blade and fillet with unthickened epoxy will smooth out the fillet and make for less sanding.

When the epoxy has cured, measure up from the tip of each blade 50½ inches, cut the rod, and add the stainless-steel ferrule to both sections (**Figure 29-26**). You may find it's necessary to sand the rod some to get the ferrule to slide over the end. Just take off a small amount and then check the fit often.

Paddle length is a personal preference and depends on the physical size of the individual, so 102 inches may not be exactly right for you. You may want to start a little longer, use the paddle some, and then cut off small amounts until you find that magic length. That way you have a truly custom paddle.

Be sure to coat everything with at least two coats of epoxy and then several coats of varnish. This will give you a double paddle that not only looks great and is exactly the right length, but was very inexpensive to boot. **Figure 29-27** is the finished paddle.

Figure 29-27

Suppliers

All the suppliers listed below I used for the boats in this book.

System Three Epoxies
3500 West Valley Highway North #105
Auburn, WA 98001
800-333-5514
www.systemthree.com
Resins and fiberglass cloth and tape

Duckworksmagazine.com
Duckworksbbs.com
Mail order for sails, foot braces, and boatbuilding supplies

Jamestown Distributors
17 Peckham Drive
Bristol, RI 02809
800-423-0030
www.jamestowndistributors.com
Stainless-steel and bronze fasteners, tools, and boat-building supplies

McFeely's
3720 Cohen Place
Lynchburg, VA 24506
800- 443-7937
www.mcfeelys.com
Stainless-steel threaded inserts and fasteners

Rockler Woodworking and Hardware
4365 Willow Drive
Medina, MN 55340
800-279-4441
Hatch cover knobs, tools, and hardware

Fine Lumber and Plywood, Inc.
9407 Brown Lane
Austin, TX 78754
512-836-8990
www.finelumber.com
Lloyd's Certified BS1088 marine plywood, a good selection of hardwoods, and a knowledgeable staff

John Henry Inc.
P.O. Box 7473
Spanish Fort, AL 36577
251-626-2288
email: scarffer@netscape.com
Scarfing attachment for Makita planer

Little Princess Plans (12 Feet)

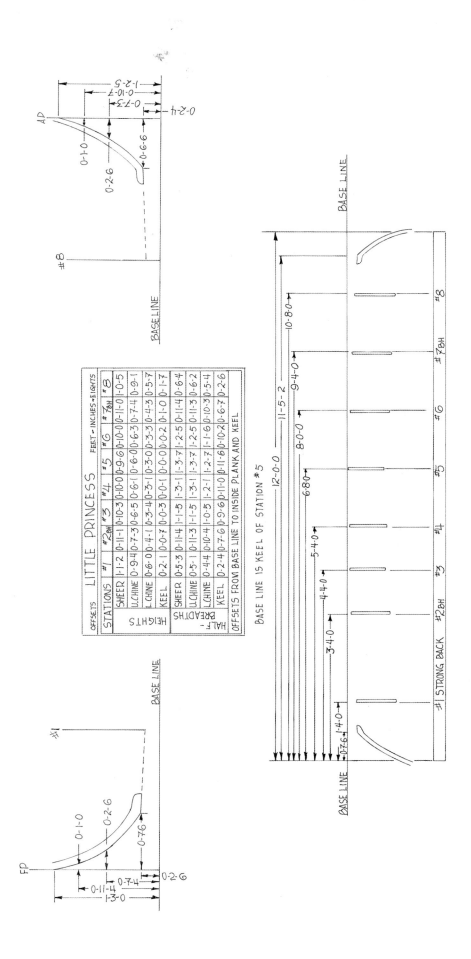

OFFSETS	LITTLE PRINCESS							FEET - INCHES - EIGHTS	
	STATIONS	#1	#2 BH	#3	#4	#5	#6	#7 BH	#8
HEIGHTS	SHEER	1-1-2	0-11-1	0-10-3	0-10-0	0-9-6	0-10-0	0-11-0	1-0-5
	U.CHINE	0-9-4	0-7-3	0-6-5	0-6-1	0-6-0	0-6-3	0-7-4	0-9-1
	L.CHINE	0-6-0	0-4-1	0-3-4	0-3-1	0-3-0	0-3-3	0-4-3	0-5-7
	KEEL	0-2-1	0-0-7	0-0-3	0-0-1	0-0-0	0-0-2	0-1-0	0-1-7
HALF-BREADTHS	SHEER	0-5-3	0-11-4	1-1-5	1-3-1	1-3-7	1-2-5	0-11-4	0-6-4
	U.CHINE	0-5-1	0-11-3	1-1-5	1-3-1	1-3-7	1-2-5	0-11-3	0-6-2
	L.CHINE	0-4-4	0-10-4	1-0-5	1-2-1	1-2-7	1-1-6	0-10-3	0-5-4
	KEEL	0-2-4	0-7-6	0-9-6	0-11-0	0-11-0	0-10-2	0-6-7	0-2-6

OFFSETS FROM BASE LINE TO INSIDE PLANK AND KEEL

BASE LINE IS KEEL OF STATION #5

Lutra One Plans (14 Feet)

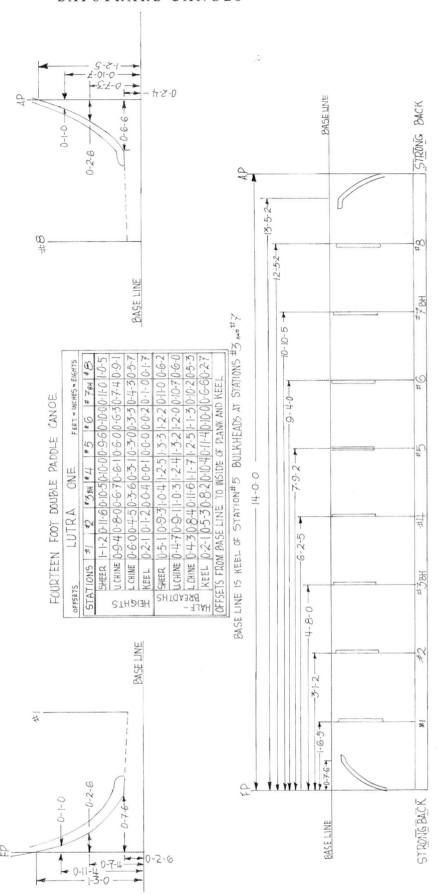

Lutra Two Plans (16 Feet)

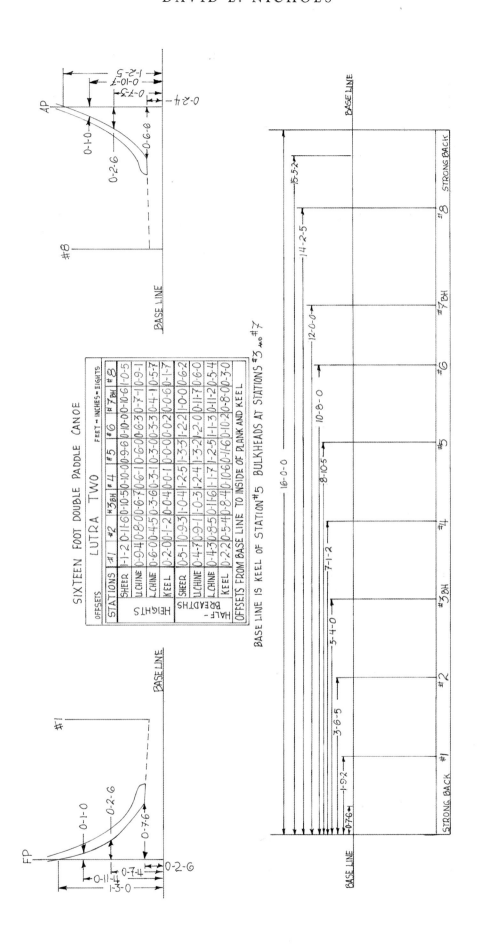